Where's Tommy?

*A Mother's Journey Through Her
Son's Traumatic Brain Injury*

Debbie Lennon

Print ISBN: 979-8-9928819-0-5
Ebook ISBN: 979-8-9928819-1-2

REVIEWS

"Tommy's story of going from a normal teenage boy to psychosis in a matter of weeks is heartbreaking. The serious mental illness that results from his head injury shows all the classic symptoms, including addiction, and plunges Tommy and his family into our fractured behavioral health system."

—Ratan Bhavnani, Executive Director
NAMI Ventura County, National Alliance on
Mental Illness Board President from 2005-2008

"This story is a raw and intimate journey into Tommy Lennon's life after he suffered a head injury in a surfing accident. Tommy was a charming, creative, funny teenager, but after the accident the changes were dramatic and scary. Debbie Lennon, his mother, offers a gripping account of his life and their family's heartbreaking experience. This story is essential reading for anyone with a loved one in need of support."

—Chuck and Marilyn Braverman
Producer and Director of *A Revolving Door*, an
award winning documentary about Tommy Lennon

"The Lennon family reminds me of a baby's mobile dangling over a baby's crib. Even touching the center piece sets all other pieces in jiggling motion. Tommy became the centerpiece of this family by necessity after his surfing accident, and his actions in turn "jiggled" everyone who loved him. Please read this book to help you understand, and join the Lennons and millions of other families who are carrying the brain injury load of care to help change the way brain injury, drug abuse and mental illness are handled in America."

—Sue Rueb
Founder of Brain Rehabilitation
and Injury Network (B.R.A.I.N.)

CHAPTER 1

HOW DID WE GET HERE?

Inside a Ventura County Courtroom, an armed guard enters a caged room with thick protective glass, followed by prisoners one at a time. With one hand on his holstered gun, the guard scans each prisoner with predator-like eyes. Finally, Tommy walks in. He is fifth in line to enter the cage and, like all the other prisoners, he's wearing a cornflower blue zippered jumpsuit. Steel chains are wrapped around his wrists and connected to his narrow waist, continuing down his legs to his ankles. His smooth tan skin, sea green eyes, and wavy blond hair pop with brilliance under the fluorescent lighting. He looks more like a movie star than a criminal.

My mind isn't comprehending what my eyes are seeing. The guard is there to protect me and the rest of society from our son. Trembling inside my own skin, I feel my left eye start flickering, continuously. I don't know how to make the involuntary motion stop. My head moves back and forth as if my wracked mind is trying to clear this image, but it won't stop.

Tommy's forehead is furrowed. He acknowledges us by raising his eyebrows, no other expression is on his face. I raise my eyebrows to acknowledge him. I have no other expression on my face. Riveted to my chair, I tighten my grip around the ends of the arm rests.

The judge brings his courtroom to order, and with an angst in his pitch, he enunciates clearly, "There will be no communicating with the prisoners whatsoever. There will be severe consequences if you do. You'll be sentenced to do jail time."

My eyes dart in every direction, fiercely trying to take in every visible detail around me. I'm insanely intent on understanding what's happening today.

The judge, rearranging his paperwork, taps it altogether on his bench, like a tall deck of playing cards.

"Thomas Patrick Lennon Jr."

Tommy rises to his feet and shuffles into the courtroom with that tangle of chains clanking at every step. He steps up to a podium that has a microphone. His back is to us.

"Mr. Lennon?"

"Yes."

The judge continues to read, "Mr. Lennon, it appears that the charges against you have been dropped. After the bailiff leads you out of my courtroom, you will be processed and released, free to go."

At the sound of the gavel, Tommy draws in an enormous breath of air. While exhaling, I can visibly see his shoulders drop down from under his earlobes as the stress leaves him and he's flooded with relief. Neither the judge nor Tommy ever go into any detail about the event that led to Tommy's arrest and charges. All we do know is, Tommy's been somehow spared. This time.

As we walk down the stairs from the courtroom, my husband Tom takes my hand, and then holds me in his arms as he has done so many times before over the years. Somehow this tragic part of our journey brings us closer together. Even when our hearts are being torn apart, the one thing that remains constant in the unpredictable unfolding of our lives, is our love.

Late that night Tommy calls collect from a payphone in Ventura. "I've been released...I know it's late. Is there any chance I could get a ride home? Thanks so much! I'll be waiting outside the courthouse."

When we see Tommy, he's wearing his street clothes. We stop the truck at the curb outside the jail next to the courthouse. Getting into the back of the truck cab, he can barely pause to say hi before starting to cry and becoming unhinged.

"Jail is so horrible! You didn't know this, but I was addicted to heroin when I got arrested, and I detoxed from it in there! I couldn't stop the shaking, sweating, the chills...and my head! If a head can explode, I thought mine was going to. I was throwing up and on the toilet without stopping for three days! My back and leg spasms were so bad, they just wouldn't stop! And no one ever checked on me, not ever! Not even to see if I was dying, which I thought I was!"

Tom and I are both stunned, speechless. The only sound penetrating the silence is our truck tires humming on the road.

But one thought keeps repeating in my mind over and over, *"How did we get here?"*

CHAPTER 2

OJAI ROOTS

O ur family moved to Ojai from Venice, California in 1974. Tom's Great Uncle Maximillian Heinrich had bought an apricot ranch here in the 1930s, and his Topa Topa View Ranch in upper Ojai introduced us to this wonderful area. Ojai, a Chumash word, which most believe means the "Valley of the Moon," was a favorite family destination for all of the Lennon families to gather. Tom's uncle, Jimmy Lennon, a Hall of Fame boxing announcer for more than four decades, was a regular visitor. As were the singing Lennon Sisters, Tom's first cousins, who appeared on Lawrence Welk's weekly television show from 1955-1968. After Uncle Max died in 1971, the families and cousins continued to gather at *our* house in Ojai, honoring their Great Uncle Max, the beautiful Ojai surrounds, and their family's traditional love of music.

Sometimes we would all fundraise for our community church and its school, and the townspeople would gather to hear the Lennon family's seamless harmonies. Sometimes they' d invite me to play my fiddle. This was the world that often surrounded Tommy and his siblings as they grew up; a world of music and laughter and making others feel happy. Young Tommy fit right in.

When Tommy was in 8th grade, all five of our children attended St. Thomas Aquinas, a K-8th grade parochial school. Tommy decided to enter the school talent show and choreographed break dance moves to the hit song 'Buffalo Girls' for himself and his two brothers, making sure each brother took a turn at showcasing their talents. Their school principal, Sister Xavior, displayed an ear-to-ear grin as she tapped her toes to the hip music. Unbeknownst to most of us, the song's lyrics are about dancing girls who perform in bars and brothels! Sister Xavior nevertheless applauded her approval and announced them the winners of the K-8th grade talent show.

And as Tommy entered high school, he'd continued to excel. As an athlete, a student, a coach for his younger brother's teams, and he had a very nice girlfriend, Carla. Everybody loved Tommy.

CHAPTER 3

THE ACCIDENT

On a cool, overcast day in late November, Tommy's friend Chris calls him and tells him, "The surf is up!" A couple hours after Chris picks Tommy up, we get a telephone call.

"Debbie! It's Chris! Tommy's surfboard skeg gashed open his forehead down through his eye and into his cheek. I don't know if it got his eye. I think it knocked him out! I got him to shore. He's bleeding a lot. An ambulance took him to the hospital in Ventura."

Emotionally reeling, I try to gather myself quickly. I can't find my purse fast enough. Grabbing the car keys off of a hook next to the back door, I run out to the barn. Frantically looking for Tom, I find him in the garage. I barge in, and by the look on Tom's face, he knows I'm about to tell him something dreadful.

"Chris just called. Tommy's been in a bad surfing accident, and he's been taken by ambulance to the Community Memorial Hospital." Tom's jaw drops open. Within seconds he shuts down his workspace. Walking at a breakneck pace back towards the house, not a word is spoken. Once in the car, Tom asks for more details.

Arriving at the hospital in record time, we rush up to the receptionist, "Our son Thomas Lennon has been in a surfing accident."

"He's already been taken into the emergency room. Go down that corridor, until you come to the end of it. You'll see Emergency written in bold red letters above the entryway."

Once there, we are led through two massive doors that have a small square window placed in the middle of each one. Hearing a bustle of activity, we peer through an opening in the sheer white curtains and see a doctor hovering over Tommy. The doctor spots us and steps outside of the sphere.

"Are you Thomas' parents? I'm Dr. Burkhart. The good news is your son is displaying coherent cognitive recall. Apparently, he was surfing big waves and, after riding one, he kicked his surfboard out and away from his body. But the rubber leash, velcroed around his ankle, snapped the surfboard back, slamming it into his right forehead, causing him to become incapacitated. Luckily, his friend brought him up and onto the shore. Otherwise, he could have drowned."

Throwing open the thin curtain, two nurses don't look up. One is holding Tommy's gaping, ragged skin open, while the other is flushing out his sandy facial wounds by spilling reddish pink liquid from a stainless-steel apparatus.

Dr. Burkhart speaks again, "The surfboard's impact did not have an effect on your son's eyesight, and the x-ray of your son's skull appears to be normal. But professionally speaking, he could have a hairline fracture that I wasn't able to detect. As luck would have it, we happen to have a very fine plastic surgeon working here today, and he will be available to work on your son within the hour." The doctor continues. "With such a substantial blow to the head, keep a close eye on him. If he experiences any eye dilation, dizziness, headaches or vomiting, call me. If everything goes smoothly, he'll know when he's up to returning to school, and so will you."

Considering the doctor's positive diagnosis and feedback, were we so foolish to assume that Tommy had been completely spared?

Hearing the words, "Knock, knock," a new figure enters the fabric circle. Dr. Burkhart introduces us. "This is Dr. Abbot, the plastic surgeon that'll be working on Tommy's facial wounds." Dr. Burkhart yields his workspace to Dr. Abbott, giving Tommy a thumbs up. "After Dr. Abbott closes your wounds, you can go home with your parents. But do take it easy for the next two or three days."

We are escorted back out to the waiting room, and Dr. Burkhart tells us, "Someone will come out and find you when they're finished."

It takes an hour and a half for the surgeon to close Tommy's wounds. A hospital attendant brings Tommy out to us in a wheelchair, appearing comfortably situated. From the waist down Tommy is covered in a thin, white opaque cotton blanket. It only slightly covers his still-sandy bare feet.

Back outside, it takes both Tom and the attendant to get Tommy out of the wheelchair and into the back seat of our car. Tom asks Tommy, "How are you doing?" Tommy's voice trails off as he mumbles 'ok'. "Are you comfortable?" Tom removes his warm fleece jacket and places it around Tommy's shoulders, pulling it closed and flipping the collar up around his neck. "This should keep you comfortable until the car heater warms up." Tommy tilts his head back and dozes off. We drive home in silence.

Throughout the rest of the day, Tommy rests and sleeps. Occasionally we wake him to check on his pupils and ask if he's feeling dizzy or nauseous. By the late afternoon our telephone starts ringing off the hook. People are asking to speak with Tommy. Taking names, numbers and messages, we thank people for inquiring. "We'll let him know that you called."

The following day, Tommy's sister, Lisa, comes home from school and informs us, "All the kids we know from the Ojai and Ventura schools are over-the-top impressed that Tommy is still alive! Tommy and Chris are being called surfing heroes, like they're total celebrities now!"

Forty-eight hours after Tommy's accident, he's begging to go back to school. "I feel fine. Even the doctor said when I feel good enough it's ok to return to school, remember?"

With seventy-two stitches keeping his gaping wounds closed, I ask him, "What if you momentarily forget about your stitches and become rambunctious and reopen the detailed work the doctor just did on your face!?"

"Mom, I'm not gonna forget!"

Tommy does seem well rested and steady on his feet. Trying to be cautious, we strike a deal with him. "If you promise to come home and rest every day after school, up until the day you get your stitches removed, then we'll give you permission to return to school tomorrow."

Breathing a sigh of relief, he eagerly replies, "Deal! I promise!"

Then one morning, with the rest of the kids in the van ready to head out to their schools, we find Tommy–with bandages still covering his wounds–smoking marijuana in his bathroom! Doing drugs of any kind is a huge red flag for us, and we're scared, angry and disappointed in him.

Between us, Tom and I decide to chalk this one incident up to perhaps just being normal teenage behavior/rebellion. But it definitely is out of character for Tommy.

Ten days later we return to Dr. Abbott's office. Greeting us with handshakes and a welcoming smile, he asks Tommy, "Well, are you ready to get all that stitching out?"

After removing one stitch at a time, the doctor comments on his own work, "The closure turned out better than I could have imagined! You've healed beautifully! It's ok to turn your head now, and show your parents."

Looking at Tommy's face, we are pleasantly surprised by the good outcome of the surgeon's work. He hands Tommy a small mirror. "As you can see, the injured skin that got pieced back together has laid down seamlessly. The impact zone on your face is still slightly swollen and bruised, but by the looks of how fast you are healing, I believe the scarring will be barely noticeable. At this point it's safe to say you can resume all of your physical activities."

Tommy can see for himself what a great job the surgeon has done. Elated with the results, Tommy asks the surgeon one more question, "So it's ok if I start surfing again?"

"Yes, you can return to surfing Tommy, and all the activities you were engaged in before your accident." When Tom and I express our heartfelt appreciation, and sincerely thank Dr. Abbott, he responds with an acute observation, "I'm also encouraging both of you, mom and dad, to fully resume your activities and routines too!"

The surgeon's advice to Tom and I proves to be easier said than done. Back home, the telephone rings. It's Tommy's girlfriend.

"Hi, Mrs. Lennon, this is Carla, is Lisa there?"

"Yes, I'll tell her you're on the telephone."

After Lisa hangs up the phone with Carla, Lisa quickly comes into the kitchen to tell us about their call. She recounts their conversation, starting with Carla's question, "Have you noticed anything different about your brother Tommy lately?"

"No, what do ya mean?"

"Well, it seems like ever since his accident, he's not been acting like himself. He's become silly, and distant."

"Silly and distant how?"

"Well, during our snack break today he took my pink flowered headband off of my head, and put it on his head. When I asked for it back, he ran off and wore it on his head all throughout our snack break. I was really embarrassed for him, and myself. Has he told you he's been hanging out with Janette and Jennifer?"

"Noooooo!"

"You know they're seniors, right?"

"Yes! The most popular, beautiful girls in their class, *and* on the Honor Roll!"

"Yes-ss! That's them! Did you know Janette just turned nineteen, and Jennifer is eighteen?"

"What does that have to do with Tommy?"

"Lisa!! Tommy's only sixteen!"

"I'm not following you."

"The two of us don't hang out after school anymore. Instead, he lets the girls drive him around wherever he wants to go! Music stores, the surf shop, out to eat."

"What do you mean? Aren't you guys going steady anymore?"

Apparently Carla just fell apart at that moment. Crying and talking at the same time, she finally managed to say, "Lisa, I really miss him. I'm crushed. Tommy is no longer showing me the respect he has always shown me."

"I'm so sorry Carla! Yeah, that really doesn't sound like Tommy. I'm not sure what to say."

"Did you know he's big-time partying on the weekends?"

"Nooo!! Really?!"

Shortly after Lisa's emotional call, Tom and I get a letter in the mail from Carla. "I care so much for Tommy, but he has really changed. It's like he's not the same person he once was. I'm seriously concerned for him and the choices he's making."

When we confront Tommy with Carla's letter, he tells us, "Yeah, I broke up with her. She's just trying to get back at me and get me into trouble."

Tommy has always been so trustworthy and level-headed that we believe him.

Shortly after receiving Carla's letter, we give Tommy permission to spend the night at a friend's house. The following morning, I pick up the boys, and on our way home I hear someone vomiting in the backseat of the van. Turning around to see who's sick, it's Tommy! His friend is laughing. I'm thinking, what a weird reaction! But then within moments, our Econoline reeks of alcohol and vomit. It was then that I understood his friend's inappropriate response.

Tommy's after school activities began to change. If he didn't have football practice or wasn't spending time with the senior girls, he'd surf, then come home and shoot hoops with his brothers and sisters. After dinner he'd do his homework, and while watching TV, he'd do sit ups, counting his reps.

Although all this can be normal activities for a teen, it's the level of his fervor and pace that I'm beginning to question. On some intuitive level, I sense something *is* different about Tommy. If I were to describe the angst, it's his momentum that I can't keep up with. It's like I'm trying to catch a train that's already left the station.

CHAPTER 4

OUR LENNON FAMILY

To help you understand how our world was changing, let me invite you into our home on a typical day in 1987...

Tom leaves for work early. I go back to sleep until 6:00 a.m. and then get up, get dressed, go downstairs, and wake up the kids. They all slip into their robotic school morning routines as I start mine. Making breakfast, then finishing sack lunches, I give them all a 5-minute warning before we are about to leave. When the time is up without a minute to spare, I give them a shout out, "Get your books! Get your backpacks! Get your lunches!" I sound more like a short order cook than their loving mom. Then with one last call, I warn them, "I'm getting in the van!" As though it's a threat, and I'd leave without one of them.

On our way to school, I turn down their music station to remind them of the day's schedule. "Tommy, you're staying after school for football drills. Lisa and Laurie, I'll be dropping you both off at your dance classes."

In a panic Laurie announces, "I forgot my dance bag! I left it at home!"

"I'll bring it to you when I pick you up." Problem solved. "Jeff, you've got a guitar lesson, and Teddy, basketball practice."

When we all finally get home around 5:30 p.m. the van door slides open, and the kids scatter in various directions all looking to enjoy what's left of their free time. Even in the busyness of family life, Tom and I always pause when returning home to greet each other with an affectionate kiss and hug. He's been home for a while after working long hours. Tom is in charge of distributing sourdough and French bread from Westlake to Santa Barbara for the Pioneer French Baking Company.

While Tom and I are visiting in the kitchen, dinner is simmering in a slow cooker. I put a green salad together, and Tom finishes off some fresh half-baked sourdough rolls in the oven. Sourdough is a major part of life in the Lennon family!

Everyone is hungry, and they are called to come and sit down for dinner. Gathering around our circular oak table, we serve up hot stew with garden fresh vegetables and (of course) sourdough bread. We share about our days with amusing, enjoyable, and occasionally serious conversations like, 'my math teacher was in such a bad mood today, she gave us all extra homework', or 'did you sign Becky's cast after she fell off of her horse?' The kids help clear the table while I whip up a little Lennon favorite–homemade fudge topping from a recipe on the back of a Hershey's cocoa tin. Drizzling hot fudge over each small helping of vanilla ice cream, our dining area falls silent except for the sounds of delicious satisfaction.

When the tabletop gets cleared and wiped down one last time, the kids sit down to start their homework. Tom, proficient in math, helps tutor in whatever subject someone needs help with.

I get organized for the following day by throwing school uniforms into the wash, writing names on lunch bags, and washing some apples from our trees. Placing an apple in each bag along with a small bag of lunch chips, I make homemade chocolate chip cookies and leave the sandwich making until morning.

Exciting, yes? Just another American family. In some ways, it was heaven and regretfully, it was short lived.

One night after dinner, we get a disturbing phone call. Picking up the receiver, I hear, "Mrs. Lennon? This is Sister Augusta. Your son Tommy is in my art class at Saint Bonaventure High School."

"Yes, hello!"

"I'm calling because I've noticed that your son is behaving differently. It's as if he's deliberately challenging authority."

I ask with concern, "Can you give me an example Sister?"

She continues, "Well, just a simple thing like keeping his shirt tucked in, which is a school rule. Today before entering my classroom, I asked him to tuck in his shirt. Instead of doing that, he pops off in a sing-song sort of way, asking me a contrary question like 'Is keeping my shirt tucked in *really* necessary Sister?' I must admit, Mrs. Lennon, because of his jovial attitude, he catches me off guard, causing me to chuckle a bit. Well, that put a smile on *his* face, compounding the problem even more! He's just gotten so silly!"

Sister ends our conversation quickly with, "I think it is imperative you and Mr. Lennon speak with Tommy as soon as possible. Tommy is admired and a very popular student. But this new behavior must be stopped! Please stress the importance of this call and obeying our school rules to Tommy, or he'll have to face more severe consequences in the near future."

Hanging up the telephone, Tommy walks into the kitchen looking for something to snack on. "Who were you talking to Mom?"

"I just got off the phone with your art teacher, Sister Augusta. She wants Dad and I to have a talk with you about misbehaving at school." Tom, overhearing our conversation, enters the kitchen.

"So, what's up Tommy?"

Tommy doesn't seem to want to look at Tom and is intently focused on shuffling through the snacks in the pantry.

"My art teacher, Sister Augusta, just called Mom. You and Mom are supposed to have a talk with me."

"About what?"

"Apparently you've become silly, and you're not keeping your shirt tucked in, which is a school rule."

"Is that true, Tommy?"

"Yeah Dad, I guess so," popping another Ritz cracker into his mouth.

"Why haven't you been keeping your shirt tucked in? You know the rules."

"I don't know, I'll keep my shirt tucked in. I'm sorry."

When Tom and I find a chance to talk privately, I reiterate what Tom already knows; my concerns regarding Tommy's unfamiliar behavior.

"Tom, too many glaring circumstances are stacking up. Carla's letter, partying on the weekend, and now with the school calling tonight, I don't know what to attribute his sudden behavioral changes to."

We decide to seek outside help. I find a therapist who's on our insurance plan and make an appointment for the three of us to meet.

When the counselor asks Tom why we are seeking counseling, he replies, "Tommy's been making some impulsive decisions. He's going through life as though there are no red lights, only green ones. It's as if he can only focus on what's immediately in front of him, and even then, he's responding inappropriately."

"Mrs. Lennon? The same question please."

"It's like he doesn't recognize when I'm upset with him for not helping out more, like he used to. He was always so willing to help one of his siblings, or do a chore, but instead, when I say something about forgetting, he breaks into a big smile like he hasn't seen me in a long time, or it's new information. We keep trying to attribute these sudden behavioral changes to being a teenager, like when he suddenly broke up with his longtime girlfriend and started hanging out with a new group at school. He went to a senior party, and after picking him up at a friend's house, he threw up in the van from drinking alcohol the night before. And then we caught him smoking marijuana in the bathroom before school one day. We couldn't believe he would do such a thing!

"When his art teacher called our home to say that Tommy is suddenly challenging authority, we thought we needed some help. Even our family rules and daily routines are getting blurred by how quickly his personality is changing."

While taking notes the therapist engages Tommy.

"So, what do you have to say about all of this Tommy? What your parents have expressed in this session?"

"I don't agree. I help at home, a lot! And so what if I broke up with my first girlfriend, it's not like I was going to marry her!" Tommy's grin floods the room with light and breaks up the tension. "I'm not being bad at school, even though a nun can pick me up by the back of my jacket and shove me up against a locker because my shirt tails are showing! So what if I don't keep my shirt tucked in, is that so baaad?"

With that, the therapist surmises, "You all appear to be reasonable people with healthy communication skills. In my many years of practice, I've experienced hostility between teens and their parents, but there isn't hostility here. I'm sensing a lot of love and respect amongst you all. So, here's what I would like to see. Mr. and Mrs. Lennon, I want you to create a clearer understanding for Tommy, so he knows the boundaries and consequences of unacceptable behavior. I want you to work on the rules and consequences all together, so that they feel reasonable and manageable for you all. It's obvious to me Tommy's a good kid! Professionally speaking, I don't see a valid reason for taking Tommy or your family on as clients."

The therapist packs up his pad of paper and pen and walks us to the door.

"There is one thing I would like to say to both of you, Mr. Lennon and Mrs. Lennon. I don't think it is necessary to give a squeaky wheel so much grease!"

CHAPTER 5

"I DON'T KNOW WHY THIS KEEPS HAPPENING!"

B ack at Saint Bonaventure High School, I began to notice a lack of eye contact and warm conversations like I used to have with other parents. Families that once loved and maybe even admired our family look down or the other way when I pass by. Maybe parents are fearful of losing their child the way we are losing ours. They seem to interpret what is happening in our family as contagious or bad parenting, perhaps both.

As confusing as Tommy's behavior is for those of us who love him, it's nearly incomprehensible for those on the outside of the immediate family looking in. Maybe it's easier to keep a polite distance than to reach out to us; maybe they don't know how to.

Whenever a church organizer would call and ask me to make a casserole for a family whose loved ones were recovering from surgery or dealing with a serious issue, I would always say 'yes'. But now, I secretly wish someone would acknowledge the sudden changes in our lives and offer to make a casserole for us because our lives are starting to fracture. We are missing the much-needed support that a church community usually provides and which we all depend on as parishioners.

As Tommy's behavior becomes more erratic and unpredictable, I feel as though the floor is moving beneath my feet. Disoriented and confused, like walking through a house of mirrors, I fumble through each day feeling like I should have my arms outstretched so that I don't bump into the next uncertainty.

Tom and I decide to call Tommy's high school and ask to make an appointment with the principal to discuss our recent concerns. The principal is put on the line immediately. Greeting us with an abrupt, "Hello!" she goes on to say, "I am completely aware of Tommy's behavior. Just yesterday he was in my office. Apparently, he tossed a chip bag into the trash but missed the receptacle. Instead of picking up the bag, he created a disturbance by laughing at himself for missing the shot. The lunch teacher asked him to pick up the bag and throw it away. He did, but not without trying to make another basket commenting, 'Swish! Yes! I just made a three pointer!' Many of our students gathered around to watch this show instead of returning to their classes after the bell rang."

I make a point of saying, "Sister, I just don't understand. Up until a few weeks ago, Tommy's always been so ready to help others and show respect."

The principal validates what I've said. "I've seen him open doors for his teachers and peers, and he'll give a helping hand when it is needed. But having already met with all of his teachers, we've surmised that Tommy, being such a likable boy, has become too much of a distraction. There's been too many silly instances which disturb our educational environment."

She clears her throat and continues, "As hard as it is to say this to you, Mr. and Mrs. Lennon, we are asking that Tommy leave Saint Bonaventure High School effective immediately. That's our final decision."

Both Tom and I are speechless. Blindsided by the principal and the faculty's decision, we muster up the courage to thank her for her time and hang up the phone. The painful reality is that our church and school community cannot help us, and we feel dismissed. If the mentors in Tommy's young life, those charged with his care, give up on him this easily, how is this ever going to get any better?

The following week we enroll Tommy in a local public high school just a few miles inland from the beach and three miles away from his old alma mater. Shortly after getting Tommy settled into his new school and routine, he comes home one day and announces that he has met a charming, beautiful girl from a well-established Ventura family.

"MOM! I met this girl today! She has long, wavy brown hair and the prettiest eyes. And her name is Felice, like Feliz Navidad!" Tommy's whole face is smiling as he talks about how they both love the beach and come from big families, how he walked her home and met her mom.

Felice and Tommy become inseparable. We begin to observe that when Tommy isn't with Felice, his poor decision making undermines any positive direction he's headed in. He cuts class to surf or stops by Felice's school to say hello when he should be at his own school attending his own classes. Tommy's new school counselor begins to call me regularly. This time he asks me to come down to the school and speak with him.

"As I've told you before, Mrs. Lennon, your son Tommy is a likable boy and quite smart. However, I don't know how he's managing to keep his grades up—he hardly makes it all the way through a day of school! He's been here for a month, but unfortunately the principal has asked me to inform you that Tommy will no longer be welcome here at Ventura High School. He's not taking his education seriously, and we are financially accountable to the state for his attendance."

When Tom comes home from work, I tell him about the visit with Tommy's high school counselor. We then interrupt Tommy, who is playing basketball with his siblings, and ask him to please come inside.

Entering the house, Tom and I sit down on a short brown leather couch by the fireplace. Tommy enters the room and sits down opposite us on a matching sofa. All of us are quiet for a moment when Tommy finally breaks the silence, "Is this about my school attendance?"

Tom replies, "No, not exactly! It's about your lack of school attendance! Your school counselor called Mom today and asked her to come down to the school. Mom was at your school today, but *you* weren't. What's going on?"

Tommy acknowledges he's been cutting class. Sorrowfully he goes to explain, "I don't know why, I just can't stay in school. I used to be able to stay in school. I just think about the things I'd rather be doing and...the next thing I know, I'm leaving to go and do them! I really don't know why! I'm sorry, I really am!"

Tommy is unable to shed any light on what's changed his behavior. We suspect something is being concealed from us, and Tom and I are deeply concerned. But we both resign from questioning him further and accept the sincere authenticity in Tommy's response. Not wanting to continue, I do continue. "Tommy, your school counselor asked me to come down to your school today so that he could inform me in person that you are being asked to leave Ventura High School."

"WHY??!!"

"Because of your absences."

"I don't understand!!! I get kicked out of school for being absent???? I do my homework! I'm keeping my grades up!"

"You're not taking your education seriously enough. I was told that the school is financially accountable to the state for each student's absence. When you're not there, they don't get the necessary funding they need to keep the school open and operating."

Tommy stands up. "Are you done speaking with me?"

We both nod. Heading back down the hallway, his shoulders are rounded forward as if his body is trying to protect his heart. We faintly hear him say, "I don't know why this keeps happening!"

CHAPTER 6

TROUBLES ON THE HOME FRONT

Tom and I weren't the only family members dealing with the new Tommy.

Not long after the accident and the changes in Tommy's behavior, each of his siblings began their own changes. Was it because of him? Were they just normal changes? Tom and I didn't know.

Lisa, at fifteen, was one year behind Tommy and doing well in school. But soon after Tommy's surfing accident, as if somehow drawn along in his wake, she too started to change and act out. Lisa began to withdraw from us, even becoming devious. Saying she was spending the night at a girlfriend's house, she instead went to parties we would have never let her go to. We have always had a delicate balance of boundaries with Lisa, and finding an appropriate consequence that wouldn't backfire into bigger problems was challenging. Lisa would never sass us, but we often feared that instead she'd just pack a bag and leave.

Tommy and his brother Jeff's unbreakable bond was swept away. At the age of thirteen, Jeff's bright skies became darkened by what seemed like an endless eclipse. Tommy chose new people, places, and partying over his relationship with his brother, causing deep wounds and feelings of alienation for Jeff. A tough decision was made. He started to diminish his involvement with Tommy and let his brother go. Jeff returned to his hometown Ojai public school system where he went on to make many new friends and excel in both sports and studies. This difficult time in Jeff's life actually opens up fields of opportunities that are allowing him to become stronger as an individual.

Ted, age eleven and still in grammar school, grew up comfortably surrounded and supported by the love and strength of our family. He always had a sense of confidence, and his older siblings would spur him on. With a great passion for both learning and sports, he became a good student and an accomplished boogie boarder. Looking to his brothers for guidance and approval, Ted soon felt confident enough to start surfing and caught on quickly. With Tommy's new behavior, however, the brotherhood Ted relied upon was gone. Ted also began acting out.

One day I received an emergency call from the principal's office demanding that I come to the school immediately. When I arrived at the office, I heard a stern, pedantic voice on the other side of the door. Knocking, I was then asked to join Ted in one of the chairs opposite Sister Bernadette's desk. Sister was so enraged that she sputtered a greeting in my direction and then went on to explain what Ted had done.

Holding a small spray bottle up, she read out loud, *"Fart Spray."* Looking back and forth between Teddy and I, she was clearly appalled. "This is a very flammable substance, and it is very disrespectful of Ted to spray it on another student." Sister stood up from her chair and instructed me to take Ted home for the rest of the day.

As we walked out to the car, I put my hand on Ted's shoulder, just for a moment, trying to ground us both. "Ted, I'm really disappointed in you...maybe you thought your actions would be funny, but they weren't. Not when you end up humiliating someone."

The ride home was quiet, until Ted giggled. "I got a nun to say the word fart." The fact our family never used that word made the whole situation even more satisfying for Ted, even though he knew he was in big trouble for having done what he did.

Laurie Beth, our youngest at age eight, showed different ways of handling the new confusion and pain in our lives. She adapted like a chameleon and tried to be the most perfect little girl by pleasing all her teachers and making everyone happy. If we could still laugh, then all hope was not lost in Laurie's world. And in her world, there was never a shortage of distractions from our new reality, because her creative imagination could invent a new life every day.

Often found daydreaming on the trampoline outside our kitchen window, I would see her just sitting there talking to herself with dramatic expressions on her face. She later told me, "When I take my cereal out to the trampoline, I pretend I live in an orphanage, and don't like the porridge."

In the grand scheme of things, most of these things may seem minor: Ted's fart spray, Laurie's unhappy orphanage life, Lisa's teenage rebellions. But at this point, Tom and I had nearly lost our ability to judge what was normal and what wasn't. We particularly were afraid of our changing relationship with Lisa, and we knew how deeply Jeff was hurting.

And we still were confused about Tommy. *Was* this just teenage behavior? Was it something we were doing wrong? I think we all were wishing that things would just go back to 'normal'.

And most confusing was that the earthly shell of Tommy's presence made it look like nothing had changed.

Determined to keep our boy in school, we hear about an alternative program called Continuation School. We enroll Tommy in the required courses to get a high school education and diploma. Three different schools in three months. All of us, including Tommy, are struggling to make sense out of all of this.

Most of his new school peers sport unusual clothing, facial hair, tattoos, and piercings; styles that were much more shocking in the early eighties than now. This was at the beginning of the Goth counter-culture. Tommy, with his knee length board shorts, surf logo t-shirts, tan face and blonde sun-streaked hair, actually stands out as clean cut.

The new school and schoolmates are foreign to what Tom and I are used to, and we struggle to be enthusiastic. Tommy appears to be doing well though. Better than Tom and me.

Although Tommy is getting to school and doing his schoolwork, we still are struggling with this different person and his unusual behavior. One day, for example, he shaved his head, his beautiful blonde surfer locks, and told us he was going to be G.I. Joe for Halloween. His unpredictable actions, even the harmless ones, were becoming more and more unsettling.

At first, we had thought that with the support of our immediate and extended family, we could handle anything. But now we realize we need some help.

Tom has a business partner who, with his wife, helped start a twelve-step program in our area called Families Anonymous. An intimate support group for anyone who loves an addict, alcoholic or, like us, someone with behavioral problems. Tom reaches out to him, and he invites us to attend a meeting.

Entering the church where the meeting is held, we see informative literature displayed on a banquet table. In one of the worship rooms, about twenty chairs are arranged in a circle, and they all fill up quickly. At 7 p.m. sharp the meeting is called to order.

A group leader welcomes everyone and invites folks to share. "We want everyone to have a chance to speak, but please, no crosstalk!"

After someone relates their experiences, and sometimes their hopes, their words just hang in the air until the next person speaks. We quickly learn that this is the meaning of "...no crosstalk!" As the sharing continues, we know we are in the right place. People sound brave, wounded, angry and grieving. Sometimes their stories are even funny in a bitter sort of way.

"As if I've nothing else better to do with my life than to listen in on my son's telephone conversations! He's been telling me 'I don't drink or use drugs anymore,' but I have to know that for sure."

Another person shares, "It's progress and not perfection! Our daughter has been on anti-depression medication for almost a month. We think the medication is finally starting to help her! Today she told us, 'I brushed my teeth for the first time in months!'"

The leader asks, "Are there any burning desires to share before we close the meeting?" With no one speaking out, he suggests, "Let's close with the serenity prayer. God, grant me the serenity to accept the things I cannot change, courage to change the things I can, and the wisdom to know the difference."

We stay afterwards to visit with a couple whose story sounds a little like ours. They inform us, "There's a telephone list on the banquet table. If you like, take one and you can add your names and telephone numbers to the newcomers list."

Driving home, Tom and I exchange our observations about the evening. We acknowledge that people talking about drug behaviors and alcohol addiction all sound similar to one another. But we don't quite hear of anyone with such a sudden behavioral change as Tommy's.

At a loss for answers, and with what we knew of Tommy's past partying and marijuana use, we decide to look further for help.

The following day, I call our county supervisor's office and ask if they could recommend an outpatient drug treatment program, one with professional counseling for teens.

"Yes! We can recommend a free, one-on-one counseling session once a week for teens. There's also free group counseling for their siblings, parents and loved ones. There are fun events that the whole family can attend. I'll give you a telephone number to call."

Tommy willingly goes to the outpatient one-on-one counseling and joins several fun activities with kids his own age. He goes to the movies, bowling, miniature golf, the beach, and roller skating. He appears to be having a blast!

But one day out of the blue, he says, "Youth group is not fun anymore. We just do the same things over and over, and I'm getting bored hanging out with people who used to do drugs and drink, and now all they talk about is being sober."

For a while we insist that he attend, but after Tommy turns eighteen, he refuses to go. We know there is nothing we can do about it since he's legally an adult.

But to tell the truth, Tommy's new school, which we had been so afraid of, has been a godsend. The half day schedule allows Tommy plenty of time for surfing in the afternoons, and it's just short enough for his new attention span. He is being respectful and cooperative and is doing well. His teachers are enthusiastic about his commitment and progress.

On the day of his graduation from the Continuation School, Tommy isn't wearing the traditional cap and gown. Instead, he's told to wear a white-collar shirt, dark casual dress pants, and a tie. He chooses to wear a new pair of black and white Converse tennis shoes with white socks, setting off his graduation ensemble.

At the event, the principal welcomes us all and addresses the audience. "Our first graduate, who we've had the privilege of knowing for the past two years, exudes light, creativity, goodwill and likability. He shows kindness and thoughtfulness to all his fellow students and our staff. Tommy Lennon, would you please come up to the podium?"

Tommy thanks the principal for his generous words and for his time at the Continuation School. While Tommy is still at the podium, his History/English teacher, Mr. Duncan, asks if he can step up to the mic and say a few words.

"I'd like to say congratulations to you, Tommy, for all of your hard work. You have been a daily example that has lifted others to excel with higher levels of effort and performance. My wife and I have a three-year-old little boy at home, and we can only hope he will grow into as fine a person as you are. Congratulations!"

Tommy, for a moment, looks like the proud young artist he'd once been as a child. When Tommy was seven years old, he entered one of his drawings into a national Kellogg's cereal box contest. A few weeks later, he received a package in the mail. Running down the hill with such exuberance, he called out, "I got a package! A package was in the mail for meee! It's from Tony the Tiger!!"

Rolled up inside was an award certificate to hang on his bedroom wall and a bright orange t-shirt with Tony the Tiger on the front. From then on, the only time Tommy didn't wear his Tony the Tiger t-shirt was when I insisted it be washed!

And now, hearing these words of praise from Tommy's high school teacher and seeing Tommy's beaming smile, Tom and I can't help but feel optimistic about his future. Perhaps this will be a new start for him.

CHAPTER 7

CHANGES

Not long after his graduation, Tommy returns home and tells us he walked into a radio station with a rap song he wrote and recorded. Introducing himself to the local DJ, Tommy was able to convince him to have a listen. "This could be the coolest song this station has played in a long time! I call it 'Fly Girl!'" Again, was it his shy, charismatic grin, bright white teeth and surfer blond hair the DJ couldn't resist?

Having a listen, he asked Tommy, "Who's the 'Fly Girl'? She's good!"

With a proud smile, Tommy replied, "Oh that's my little sister, Laurie!"

The DJ loved the recording and played it on his radio show. "Call in and tell me what you think of this new recording artist!" Then at the end of his show he announced, "This looks like a hit!"

Though she is over-the-top excited that Tommy is on the radio, Felice still encourages him to make a regular income by getting a full-time job. After a few inquiries, he lands a job delivering newspapers in his pale blue V.W. Bug. His route is in the local neighborhoods in and around Ojai.

Starting in the wee hours, seven days a week, people wake up to their morning newspapers on their porches, delivered by Tommy. Occasionally he'd get a telephone call from the newspaper manager telling him, "Lennon! You skipped a house! They're not happy about it! Get one out there right away!" Tommy writes down the street address and quickly redelivers it by knocking on the door and personally handing the late newspaper to his customer. With his polite, apologetic manner, Tommy is often rewarded with an extra tip while being told, "You're a good kid!"

Tommy likes his newspaper route and its generous pay. It also leaves him plenty of time to surf, spend time with Felice, and attend art classes at our local Ventura College.

Thinking about learning how to silk screen clothing, Tommy says to Felice, "I'd like to open my own business and design t-shirts."

"Well Tommy, let's look into what it would take to bring that dream to fruition!"

The first step they take is to get an official business license. When asked to file a fictitious name, Tommy calls his creative works, Mind Body and Soul. Running that name in the local newspapers for a required amount of time, he hopes no one else has taken the name, and they haven't. It's his!

Tommy draws his first t-shirt design with a fine black ink pen on the back of a white t-shirt, a delicate profile of an African American girl with cornrow braids, long beautiful eyelashes, full lips, and a feminine ethnic nose. On the front of the shirt where a pocket would be, he draws a planet with his business name, Mind Body and Soul, inside it.

Tommy and Felice take his first design to a professional silkscreen artist in Ojai. The t-shirts turn out beautifully, and his brother Jeff begins selling them like hotcakes at his high school and down at the beach. Jeff even gets backlog orders!

Tommy and Felice are doing quite well, and Tom and I are quite happy.

Then Tommy enrolls in a second art design class at the college and comes home to tell me that he saw a girl who looks shockingly like the girl he had drawn on the back of his first t-shirt. I can see that he's really taken aback by how similar the two beauties are. It's like she could step into the profile on his t-shirt, the way Alfred Hitchcock stepped into his profile at the beginning of each episode of his 1960s television show.

Her name is Kim, and she had signed up at the same college as him to earn credits to become a preschool teacher. Knowing he's met his Mind, Body, and Soul-Mate, Tommy quickly loses his feelings for Felice and breaks things off with her. Without Felice keeping him on track, however, he soon drops his art class, his t-shirt business, and his newspaper delivery job. Using the last of his money, Tommy asks Kim out on a couple of dates.

Then he asks if he can bring Kim home to our house for dinner and a movie. "I want you all to meet her!"

Knowing that he is head over heels crazy about her, we enthusiastically say, "Yes, of course!"

Their love continues to grow, and Kim introduces Tommy to her family. Soon afterwards Tommy asks Kim to be his wife. They seal their commitment with a paper ring from a bubblegum cigar that Tommy gets from a candy counter, but he promises her, "I'll give you the real version soon!"

Kim, still going to school, also starts a new part time job working at an Alzheimer's facility near our home. It's not a convenient location for her to drive to from her parent's house in Oxnard. When Tommy asks us if he and Kim can move in together into a structure on the hillside above our family swimming pool, we give them the ok. Soon after Kim tells Tommy about a well-paying, part time job opening as a custodian and handyman at the same facility. Tommy applies for the job and gets hired on the spot!

After a few weeks, Tommy comes home from work one day with some bad news. While doing his usual rounds and routines, helping out wherever needed and making up empty beds, Tommy impulsively lays down, "for just a second". His manager discovers him asleep in one of the rooms and begins yelling at him in anger. Tommy jumps from a deep slumber onto his feet, but his manager had already fired him. "I couldn't help myself," Tommy explains, "I was so tired!"

Being fired from his job only causes more confusion for Tommy. He feels what he did wasn't all that bad and that people shouldn't get so mad at him. "I think he should have given me another chance. It was all just a misunderstanding."

Choosing the right solutions to new problems seems to be getting more difficult for Tommy, causing further frustration and more misunderstandings. He feels like he's being picked on, which is very unlike Tommy. For sixteen years he was so used to things going so well for him, there was very little upset in his life or ours. Perhaps he has a sense he is losing himself, but of course he doesn't know why, and neither do we.

After being together for well over a year, Tommy asks if the four of us can all sit down for dinner. I notice Tommy is extra attentive with Kim, pulling out her chair when we sit down to eat, asking her multiple times if she needs anything.

Then out of the blue, Tommy says, "Mom, Dad, we have an announcement!"

"We're pregnant!" Kim says with her perfectly white 1950s Pepsodent smile beaming at us across the table.

Tom and I jump out of our chairs and hug them, as they tell us they are due at the beginning of August!

"More than anything in the world, I want to take care of my family the way you've taken care of us," Tommy says to his dad as they embrace. "How old were you when you had me?"

"Twenty-five! Three years older than you, Tommy!"

Sitting back down to finish our dinner, I'm brimming with a special joy that only a grandparent knows.

"I'm so happy for you both," I say, squeezing Kim's hand. "I know you'll be amazing parents, and fun too!"

Tommy laughs and says, "Yeah I mean, all the responsibilities that come with being a father kinda scare me, like how do I do this? But I also feel sorta fearless."

Tommy turns to Kim and says, "I can hardly wait to meet our baby! I know it'll be healthy and beautiful, just like its mama."

On August 2, 1993, Elijah Thomas Lennon arrives and doesn't disappoint! His sparkling brown eyes reflect light, bouncing love arrows toward us all. It's as if the winged messenger Cupid, the son of Venus, goddess of love, arrives and seals us all into the same floating bubble that's headed into the cosmos.

Elijah's smooth, soft chestnut brown curls are exquisite! His full delicate lips resemble his dad's, and his little ears look hand-sculpted by Michelangelo. The mix of Tommy being a quarter Irish, a quarter German, a quarter English and a quarter Jewish, combined with Kim's African-American heritage by way of Bermuda, has produced a beautiful child, little 'Jah'.

As their new little family unit begins to settle into life altogether, Tommy takes full time, on-call work with a construction company. He likes the on-call setup and sees potential for longterm opportunities.

Kim loves being a mom and raising their new baby with her sisters-in-law and their new babies. Elijah, a cheerful cherub with a sunny disposition and great exuberance, spends most of his days growing up side by side with his two cousins. They are so close in age, that for one month out of each year, Elijah and his cousins are all the same age. With life flowering like the springtime sweet peas trailing about the white picket fence just outside our front door, life is good on Camp Chaffee Road.

By the time Elijah is six months old, Kim and Tommy are financially solid enough to rent a quaint, airy bachelor apartment in downtown Ojai close to family, parks, markets and their favorite burrito shop! Truly living the quintessential Ojai small town family life, they are all in good spirits whenever we see them for family dinners or when we stop at their house to spend time with our sweet grandson, Elijah.

CHAPTER 8

A WAYWARD WIND BLOWS

A few months later, while we are upstairs packing for a family trip, Tommy calls with an urgent tone in his voice and asks if we'll be home because he needs to speak with us. But before I can respond, he hangs up, and within thirty minutes, he's at our house.

"I really need a place to stay until Kim and I can work things out," he says.

"Tommy! We have a family trip planned, remember? We're taking Ted and Laurie to visit Lisa and her family in Hawaii. What happened with Kim? Is everything ok?"

He looks tired. "I don't want to talk about it right now, Mom. Can you please just tell me if I can stay?"

Tom and I exchange concerned glances.

"I suppose you can stay in the old teardrop surf trailer," Tom says. "It's been cleaned."

"Yes, and we'll fill its pantry and the small fridge with food and lock up the house, except for the back entry door to the bathroom and laundry room. That's what we can do for you right now."

"No, that's great! Thanks Mom and Dad," Tommy sighs deeply and hugs us both.

With our flight leaving for Hawaii the next morning, we don't have much time to talk with Tommy about what's happened. Our family only knows that Tommy and Kim have had a very big misunderstanding.

Several days into our vacation, my older sister calls and tells me, "Mom has been taken to the hospital. She is declining rapidly. How soon can you return home?"

Quickly packing our things, Tom calls the airline to exchange our tickets so that we can catch a redeye flight that evening. After traveling for many hours, we all arrive home at three in the morning.

What we see as we enter the house is hard to believe. The barrage of sensory information coming in all at once is short circuiting my brain. Our kitchen is littered with old food on every plate, bowl, cup, glass, pot, pan, and utensil. Beverage containers are overturned and spilled on the furniture and flooring. The refrigerator, freezer and pantry are completely emptied. Soup cans, food boxes, and freezer containers are all over the kitchen floor and flung about the house. Cigarette butts and sunflower seed husks have been dropped and flicked everywhere, even on windowsills.

Feeling dazed and confused in our exhaustion and unable to think clearly, we do a walk-through and discover that many of our most valuable personal belongings are gone. My wedding ring and other family jewelry pieces...gone. Teddy's television and Nintendo games, for which he had worked hard and saved his money...gone.

Before leaving on our trip, Tom had shut off the water to two of our three toilets. They are now reeking of raw sewage because they had been used like outhouses. Teddy discovers Tommy asleep in *his* bed and wakes him up.

"What the hell, dude?!!!!!!"

Half asleep and slurring his words, Tommy tells Ted, "Yeah, people just kept coming over. I didn't know what to do, I didn't even know who they were."

Tom calls the police.

Two uniformed police officers arrive at our house and survey the situation. They basically say, "Unless you have a restraining order against your son, he could be in your home and have all the guests he wants. Other than the thefts, which we are making reports on, no other laws have been broken. We suggest you start checking the pawn shops in this area as soon as possible, and you may recover your jewelry and other stolen articles. Oh! And FYI, your stove was used to liquify heroin rocks into an injectable substance, which is why all of your spoons have been blackened."

After the police leave, it's clear Tommy is under the influence of something, but we don't know what. Unable to participate or help us with the clean-up, we send him back to the trailer we originally left for him before we went on vacation.

As dawn breaks, we desperately need to sleep, but soon after my sisters call to say, "Mom is dying. See you as soon as you can get here."

Drinking a cup of coffee and packing an overnight bag at the same time, I get dressed and leave for the hospital. The car needs gas. Pulling off the highway, a gasoline attendant fills my car with petrol. I see a telephone booth and call Tom.

"How are things going?"

"We're slowly getting it put back together."

"Where's Tommy?"

"He left right after you."

"Do you know where he went?"

"No, he didn't say. I couldn't ask."

Feeling so grateful I made it in time to say goodbye to Mom, I greet both of my sisters at the hospital. Our oldest sister, being a registered nurse, informs us, "Mom can still hear you even though she's unable to speak. I think it's best if we each take a turn to go in and say whatever it is that's on our hearts."

Rocked by all the events since boarding that red-eyed flight home from Hawaii, I found myself just wanting to protect our mom and say what I thought she'd want to hear, "We all loved you so much, Mom." And as I'm speaking, I am feeling relieved she doesn't know about Tommy and all we had just experienced. Watching our mom in the last moments of her life, a startling thought hits me hard—have we lost our boy Tommy too?

Some weeks after my mom's death, Kim stops by unannounced and tells us something has gone terribly wrong with Tommy.

"A few months ago, I got a call from a dear highschool friend, and she invited me and Tommy over for dinner with her and her boyfriend, Eric. I didn't know anything about this guy, and I really wish I had..." Kim's voice cracks and she fights to hold back tears.

"Tommy didn't know...I know this isn't him!"

My mind is reeling, making up stories about what could possibly be happening. "Kim, please tell us what's going on!"

"Tommy did heroin with Eric, and he hasn't stopped since! It's completely out of control!"

Tom hugs Kim as she sobs in his arms. Baby Elijah pulls himself up and is standing at our coffee table. Amused by his newest accomplishment, he is smiling. Looking at his mom, waiting to hear her routine response and encouragement, he bounces with delight. But there is no laughter, no applause today. Feeling frightened, he begins to cry, and I swoop him up in my arms and walk with him near the windows to point out the birds in the tree. Maybe I need a distraction too. My face feels numb and tingling as fear pulses through my veins. I set up the couch with pillows and Elijah's blankie and put Sesame Street on the

TV, hoping that will keep him cozy in the world of kids for a little while.

"Eric did it, he shot Tommy up the first time, and after that he was hooked! It's really bad! And now his body is starting to deteriorate. He said he couldn't handle the heavy labor of construction, so he dropped to part time, but then he just spent every dollar on drugs, and most of the time he didn't even make it home."

There are no words for a moment like this. "I'm so sorry Kim," I hear myself say. "We want you to know we are here for you, whatever you and Elijah need."

"Well I was desperate and called my dad, so we're staying with him now." We know Kim's dad is a recently widowed, retired Naval officer, a man of sustenance and caring determination, and Kim knows she can rely on him.

"I tried to keep us together as long as I could, I promise! I just snapped into my routines, making breakfast, cleaning the apartment, taking Elijah to the park, making lunch and then eventually dinner. I feel like a terrible mom because I know I'm not totally there for Elijah! I am worried all the time and just going through the motions and looking forward to sleeping every night just so I can get a break from everything that's happening! So that's when I called my dad. I'm so sorry, I know this is terrible to hear!"

We are all silent for a moment as the voices of Big Bird and Cookie Monster talk about sharing on the TV.

"Now he's been sleeping outside my dad's house, insisting to be near me and the baby. Every once in a while, I feel so badly for him that I allow him to come inside and see Elijah. Tommy looks at Elijah and just starts sobbing. He says over and over again, 'I'm sorry, I'm so sorry Kim! I don't know why I turned out so different from everyone else in my family.'"

Hesitating for a moment, she continues, "I didn't want to be the one to tell you guys, I think he's panhandling now to pay for his addiction. I'm so shocked by what's happening! How can we be such a loving family one moment and like shattered glass the next?"

CHAPTER 9

TRYING TO MAKE THINGS WORK

S oon after that fateful conversation and turn of events, Kim tells us that her father Essex had begun missing his larger family in the South. He asked Kim if she and Elijah would come and live there with him, so he could house and feed them until Elijah is old enough for her to start working. Then he could babysit.

Kim was understandably tempted to have so much built-in support, but she told her dad that she is still hopeful she and Tommy can somehow get through this terrible time. Maybe the insanity could end as quickly as it began? Kim tells her father that she'll remember his offer, but she was going to stay and give this her all.

Meanwhile we discuss with Kim if she and the baby would want to move in with us. But tragically we all come to a deflating agreement on how difficult it would be if Tommy assumes he can just return to his family home and be with his own family anytime he wants. This would most likely mean him returning home even when he's high, which would mean upheaval and crisis for us all.

With financial assistance Kim finds a one-bedroom apartment for rent about ten minutes from our house, but even with us being close by, she finds caring for the baby and taking care of all of her responsibilities without a partner too much to handle.

Just before Elijah's second birthday and with sad acceptance, Kim declares, "The only way I can move forward is to let my father help me raise Elijah. The baby and I are going to move to Birmingham, Alabama. It's the only way I know how to begin a new life."

Having made her decision to move 1800 miles away, we vow to remain in each other's lives, promise to call, write letters, and visit in person whenever possible. With hugs and endless kisses, we are all left living this tragic reality.

And Tommy, having already lost himself, is now losing the most precious people on this earth, his own family. When Tommy finds out that Kim and Elijah have already moved to Alabama, his heart shatters and he continues to deteriorate and spiral down into despondency. He's lost his beloved son and his "Mind, Body and Soul-Mate."

CHAPTER 10

AN ANSWER?

Tommy decides that moving away from the familiar haunts of Ventura County might make it easier on him to stay clean. He chooses to relocate to Venice, California, the familiar hometown of his early childhood. Sadly, within a couple weeks the police stop him and start questioning him about panhandling. Upon searching him, they find marijuana in his possession, and Tommy gets arrested and thrown into the Twin Towers Jail in Los Angeles on illegal drug possession charges.

"Hello, Mr. Lennon?" says a friendly voice on the phone. "I am a forensic psychiatrist working with your son, Tommy, at Twin Towers Jail. I noticed the last name Lennon, and coincidentally Tyler, who must be your nephew, goes to my church! Small world. Anyway, Tommy gave me permission to call you guys, and I just can't make sense of such a nice kid from such a good family having Tommy's history of arrests! I wonder if you and your wife can provide me with a detailed health history about your son. Has Tommy ever suffered any severe blows to the head?"

"Yes!" Tom replies, "In a surfing accident when he was sixteen years old."

"Listen, I had a former patient that reminds me of your son. This kid, a high school senior, accepted into a university on scholarship, went on a rock-climbing expedition during his spring break. He fell and seriously injured his head. His personality changed drastically overnight. His daily school attendance became irregular, and he started using drugs. Years later, the boy was doing well to hold down a job working at McDonald's."

The psychiatrist continues, "Traumatic Brain Injury symptoms can manifest in several ways, depending on where the injury has occurred. Symptoms can include bipolar disorder, schizophrenia, lack of impulse control...which often leads to drug abuse, heightened sexuality and sudden anger outbursts. Sadly, few people are ever the same after a TBI. I suspect that Tommy has an undiagnosed Traumatic Brain Injury."

Strange as it may seem, this was really the first time it occurred to Tom and I that Tommy's behavior could be due to his head injury. And although the news was not good in terms of a prognosis for the future, it actually made us feel hopeful to at least have some explanation.

We continued to stay in touch with the psychiatrist on a regular basis. But we couldn't find a professional in the criminal or mental health fields that would or could validate and acknowledge that Tommy had sustained a Traumatic Brain Injury in his surfing accident. The system always came back to the mental health field, which does not include TBI.

CHAPTER 11

HOMELESS

Soon after getting released from the L.A. Twin Towers Jail and returning to the streets of Oxnard, we receive a collect call from Tommy.

"Dad! I need help! I got hit in the eye with a cement rock by a kid messing around with a slingshot. I'm bleeding, and I can't see out of my eye!!!!!"

"Should you hang up and call 911?"

"No, please come get me."

"Where are you?"

Tommy is weeping and disoriented but able to give Tom directions on how to find him.

Tom calls an eye specialist's office before heading out of the house and explains the situation to the receptionist. "I can schedule an emergency appointment within the hour for your son. Will that be enough time for you to get here?"

"Yes, please!"

Tom leaves immediately, and I stay behind in case Tommy calls again. The hours seem to pass like a very slow moving train that never picks up speed. Finally, just as the last light is fading over Red Mountain, I see Tom's headlights coming up the driveway. Tommy slowly enters the house with a patch over his eye and immediately falls asleep on the couch with hardly a word. Meanwhile Tom fills me in on the day.

"I went to Oxnard and found Tommy living inside a big cardboard box in an alleyway, Deb." Tom's voice fades, and I can tell he's trying not to cry. "It's like any of the hopes or dreams I had left for him were just *gone* in that moment."

After being seen by the specialist and getting the proper treatment, the doctor put a patch over Tommy's eye and told him he had to wear it for several days. He also told Tom that several follow up appointments would be needed, as this injury will require significant time to heal.

Tommy lives with us until the specialist feels his eye is healed well enough to come in for a final eye exam. Inviting the three of us into his consultation room, the doctor hands Tommy a small mirror and addresses Tommy directly. "If you look at both of your eyes, it's apparent one eye is different from the other. The injured eye is more dilated with very little of the blue green color remaining around it. Tommy, your field of vision cannot be improved with contact lenses or prescription glasses. Unfortunately, I wasn't able to save your vision. You're legally blind in your left eye."

This verdict is a blow to Tommy and to us. Feeling sick to my stomach, I observe Tommy is barely able to take the next step forward to exit the door. His shoulders slouch under the heavy burdens of his life. He doesn't come back home with us, but instead chooses to return to Oxnard to live in the appliance box, where he is apparently an easy target for arrests.

Tommy tells us that when the police see him, he gets searched, and they almost always find something illegal like being under the influence, drug paraphernalia, or pot in his possession. Because Tommy doesn't want to cooperate with the arrests (feeling he's done nothing wrong other than against himself), he often gets struck by a baton and is sometimes severely beaten or tasered. Then he's hauled off to jail for resisting arrest, even though sometimes his pockets reveal no evidence of an illegal substance or paraphernalia.

Chapter 12

Pleading Guilty

Regularly appearing before the same judge, Tommy *always* pleads guilty to the charges, whether he's guilty or not. When we ask him about pleading guilty to charges when he's not guilty, he replies, "I know how to do time. I'm told exactly how many days I'm going to serve and the exact date I get out. I just get overwhelmed with the details of going through a trial."

Tommy's condition and behavior are a challenge not only to him and us, but also to doctors, nurses, social workers, police, public defenders, the mental health workers, the government programs and the judges that regularly interact with him. Tragically, his jail sentences grow from days, into months, and eventually years.

We are soon confident that, indeed, the Twin Tower Jail psychiatrist's informal diagnosis of a TBI is the missing piece in this heartrending mystery. We know now that Tommy isn't just a derelict young person-turned-addict who can't learn a lesson. Because an adult brain isn't fully developed until the age of twenty-five, and Tommy's brain development was interrupted at the age of sixteen, Tommy is a man-child trying to do the very best that he can with the hand he's been dealt.

Frequently calling home and begging us to please explain why things turned out so differently for him than for anyone else in our family, the answer is starting to formulate from a watery mass of confusion, while we desperately search for more information on Traumatic Brain Injury.

When Tommy is doing well and off of the streets, we re-engage in a quality of life we all embrace. Hosting family and friends for rounds of volleyball games, barbecues, and swimming, it's as if we are celebrating the simpler times resurfacing with some distortion, like viewing my hand underwater.

When Tommy isn't doing well, it seems that even on the brightest of days, blue skies might as well be cloudy gray. The dread of the unknown...where's Tommy? Is he safe, fed, and housed? Tom and I are tortured by these thoughts daily, until eventually I call our therapist and set up an appointment for us.

When she returns my call she informs me, "You and Tom need a consistent quality of life that you've been missing out on for some years now. Al-Anon will help you find a way to begin to accept the uncertainty that has become a way of life for you and your loved ones. I am going to recommend that you and Tom and Tommy's siblings find a twelve-step meeting nearby, called Al-Anon." Tearing a piece of paper away from my grocery list, I write down the name.

When Tom and I and a few family members attend our first meeting, we listen to people share their personal stories about their loved ones' alcohol use or substance abuse or both. They express how their own lives have become unmanageable, and we can relate to that. Sometimes we attend the ninety-minute meeting once a week, and sometimes twice a week. In the worst of times when we are barely hanging on by a thread with the hope that Tommy is still alive, we have actually attended three meetings in one day.

Through working the Al-Anon program, we begin to find peace of mind 'in spite of unsolved problems'. But then just when we hit a point of regaining some balance in our lives, we hear Tommy crying into the telephone, "Mom, Dad...I need your help."

CHAPTER 13

WHAT'S METHADONE?

"**I** don't want to be homeless and addicted to anything anymore," Tommy cries. "I just want to live at home and be close to my family. Will you help me get into a methadone program?"

"What's methadone?"

"A legal substitute for heroin."

Our first thought is, anything that lifts you out of the life and lifestyle of a heroin addict, we'll look into. Not knowing where to turn, I call our county supervisor's office, and the receptionist gives me the number to a local methadone program.

"Oxnard Methadone Clinic, how may I help you?" I step into a conversation about a subject that I know nothing about.

"Hello, we just heard about methadone from our son. He asked if we could help assist him in getting into a methadone program. To be honest, we don't even know what methadone is?"

"Methadone is a synthetic narcotic typically used to reduce pain. It is a controlled substance, so it can have a potential for abuse and addiction, too."

"Ok. How does your program work?"

"To qualify for methadone maintenance, your son has to come into the clinic and sign up for the program. He can pick up a registration form 7am-5pm, seven days a week. Then he'll need to get clean from heroin for seventy-two hours. When he's accomplished that, he should return with his health information to get his first dose of methadone."

Tom thought if we could find a methadone program along with a rehabilitation program where Tommy might live, we could try and get him clean and as far away as possible from the heroin haunts of Oxnard.

Tom asks his parents if we can let Tommy detox in their vacation house near Escondido, three hours south from our house. His folks don't hesitate for a second to say, "Yes! We think you've come up with a very good plan. We'll be praying that this is the answer you've been looking for."

Tom finds a methadone program near his parent's getaway house. He's told the same information we'd received from the Oxnard program. The receptionist in the Escondido program reiterates about getting clean and staying off of heroin for three days before qualifying for his first dose of methadone.

Tom gives the receptionist Tommy's name and says, "He will be there to register tomorrow, early afternoon." After getting the details we need from the methadone clinic, the receptionist suggests a sober living program she knows of in their area.

Tom thanks the receptionist and calls to speak with the sober living program's director.

"Hello, my name is Tom Lennon. Our son will be going into a methadone program nearby. Can he be on methadone and also be accepted into your sober living home?"

The owner quickly responds, "We get guys in here all the time that are in the methadone program. We even provide transportation for our guys to go get what they call their 'medicine'. If your son would like us to hold a bed for him, we have one available."

Then the director explains the sober living situation to Tom. "Here's the deal, Tom. Your son would have to agree to take a tour of our facility and commit to the twelve-step program Narcotics Anonymous. He has to take his sobriety seriously if he wants to live here, and that's it! Sounds easy, but recovery is a challenge, one day at a time. We'll look forward to meeting you."

When Tommy telephones us later that evening, Tom tells him about the detox requirement to get into the methadone program and about the sober living house that he found for him to live in. "If you can agree to all of this, we'll pick you up early tomorrow morning and make the trip out to Papa and Lolly's Escondido house."

We hear an emotional quiver in Tommy's voice, "Mom and Dad, thank you. Please thank Papa and Lolly, too."

Early the next morning, we meet Tommy at the dilapidated cardboard box in the alleyway in Oxnard. Getting into our car he speaks with a slur, as though he were almost too tired to talk.

"I just used heroin. I am afraid of going into detox before getting down to the house." Once again Tom and I look at each other not knowing what to say. I'll never forget the look of sorrow in Tom's eyes. It all feels so surreal.

We stop at a gas station restroom so Tommy can change into the clean clothes we brought him. Within moments of returning to the car, his weakened body is already sprawled across the back seat. His unkempt hair stands out against the clean white cotton pillowcase his head lays on. Drifting in and out of sleep, it's more than apparent he is in desperate need of help.

Arriving in Escondido, we go straight to the methadone program, and Tommy fills out the necessary paperwork to begin methadone treatment after detoxing. Driving a short distance from the methadone facility, we arrive at the sober living house. Someone friendly steps across the threshold and says they've been expecting us. We are shown the four-bedroom, two-bathroom house. There's a washer and dryer, the floors are vacuumed, and the kitchen sink area is clean and free of dirty dishes. Across the room, in front of two long couches, is a console television with a record player inside of it playing Elvis Presley's "Return to Sender". There are men's health and sports magazines neatly sprawled across a wide teakwood coffee table.

Stepping into the garage, there's a professional weight lifting set in the corner and a punching bag close to the center of the room. Out in the backyard is a croquet game. It's all set up and ready to play on wheat colored dry grass. A picnic table is shaded by a red umbrella. There are white plastic arm chairs with tiny white tables next to them, and ashtrays are strategically placed on all the flat surfaces.

When the director asks Tommy, "Well, what do you think of the place?"

Tommy responds, "I like it. The residents seem friendly. Yeah, I think I could do this!"

While filling out the necessary paperwork for the board and care facility, the three of us know that the clock is running out on Tommy. He is going to need his heroin before nightfall. With short farewells, we focus on getting back to the house and the detox we are all dreading.

Two days into detox Tommy is violently ill with drenching sweats, vomiting and dry heaves. Tom then spots Tommy trying to leave the property. "Hey! Where are you going?"

"I need to get a little bit of the drug to ease this pain."

Tom simply says no and reminds Tommy that he is almost through with the worst part. Tommy tries to leave anyway, but in his weakened state Tom is able to stop him and take him to the ground. Tom laying on Tommy and holding his arms down while Tommy struggles to get away seems so futile, but in this moment it's the most loving thing that

Tom could do for our son, hoping he would come to his senses and not leave.

"Ok Dad, you're right! I'll go back inside the house and try to sleep through this."

Fifteen minutes after telling us what we wanted to hear, we see Tommy walking halfway down the long, steep driveway to leave the property. Heading towards the main road, he instantly catches a ride, as if the getaway car was planned and waiting for him in advance.

Just before sunset Tommy returns to the house. "I'm sorry. I just had to get enough medicine to ease the pain. But I came right back! I needed such a small amount. I couldn't believe the guy just gave it to me."

With a look of confusion on both of our faces, we ask him, "How do you know where to go? How do you know who to ask? You got back here so fast!"

He hesitates as if deciding whether to blow his cover, but Tommy then answers our questions.

"We all know who we are. All dirty and skinny. Some people look like they're anorexic, and their sunken cheekbones give them away. It's pretty obvious too when people have needle marks and sores on their arms and legs. Anyway, I don't want to talk about it anymore."

As he's talking, I notice a high end fashion magazine on the coffee table. On the front page, a model sports a beauty trend called "heroin chic grunge," promoting heroin as if it was cool during the Kurt Cobain days before he committed suicide! It's insane to think the fashion industry will do things like this to sell their magazines, and yet they show no accountability for their lack of sensitivity to the real struggles of addiction.

One more long day of withdrawal symptoms later, Tommy finally qualifies for the methadone program and the sober living house. At

7 a.m. sharp, showered and shaved, Tommy hands in his paperwork at the methadone program. We find chairs and sit down. Waiting for Tommy's name to be called, there are people in there looking cleaned up, but with the same angst of anticipation in their eyes as our boy.

Right at the designated time we hear, "Lennon? Thomas Patrick Lennon Jr.?"

As Tommy steps up to the distribution station, a technician puts on a pair of thin, blue, rubber gloves, and pours liquid from a clear glass bottle into a tiny opaque plastic cup. We watch Tommy drink his first dose of methadone.

Later, he doesn't appear to be at all doped up, like when we picked him up at the cardboard box to bring him here.

Our plans to take Tommy and his belongings to his new "home" are disrupted when he declares, "I'm not going to move into the sober living house. I need to be at home with you guys and family."

Tom, continuing to drive toward the group home anyway, is hoping that the director will encourage Tommy to stay since he's already registered at the nearby methadone clinic. But once we pull up in front of the house, Tommy refuses to get out of the car. "I'd rather be homeless and on methadone than live with strangers in strange surroundings."

Emotionally, physically, and spiritually drained, I begin to internally rage. *Do you really think we have nothing better to do than to get jerked around by your indecisiveness, every time you change your mind!!!!????* My blood is boiling! My brain feels like it's going to explode. But somehow, and I don't know how, I manage to stay silent and so does Tom. I think of the saying, "Fatigue makes cowards of us all." Tom and I are so tired, so frustrated, we feel stupid. Maybe I should have spoken aloud.

Back home Tom takes Tommy to sign up at the methadone program in Oxnard. We take turns driving him to get his daily dose. If he isn't there exactly at 7 a.m., the medicine will not be issued for that day. We watch the clock more closely than Tommy. A couple weeks into our routine, one afternoon Tommy doesn't return home. We later get a call from him saying, "I'm not coming home, I'm gonna live back out on the streets again."

Soon after Tommy's call, we attend an Al-anon meeting. A guy we had never seen before comes up to us after the meeting and says, "I don't know if you know this, but some heroin addicts use methadone and heroin at the same time. It helps keep the addict's heroin costs down, but it can lead to low bone density later in life and lots of other side effects too. Maybe it's for the best that your son is not on methadone."

Soon rearrested for having marijuana in his pocket, Tommy is standing before the same judge he usually sees and the judge barks at him, "Lennon! DOING THE SAME THING EXPECTING DIFFERENT RESULTS IS THE DEFINITION OF INSANITY. I'm sick of seeing you in my courtroom! You're stuck on a treadmill going nowhere! You've had one offense after another for so many years, I'm going to give you an opportunity to help yourself. Instead of doing jail time, I'm sentencing you to a drug rehabilitation program, but under one condition...If I ever see you in my courtroom again, I'm sending you to prison."

This is the first time we've heard the word prison because Tommy has only ever been sentenced to jail. Hanging prison over Tommy's head is a serious threat. What if he isn't successful in the rehabilitation program? How could anyone be sent to *prison* for Tommy's types of behavior? These were the questions reeling in my mind.

A couple of days after Tommy's arrival at his new sober living home in Santa Barbara, we get a phone call from the program director.

"Your son Tommy climbed out the bathroom window and left the program. Since Tommy is court ordered to serve time here, I've already called the police and reported him missing."

A couple of hours later, we get another call from the program. "Mrs. Lennon, I'm calling to tell you the police located your son, and he's been taken into custody."

Appearing in court before the same judge that had sentenced him to the rehabilitation program, the judge calls Tommy to the stand.

"Lennon, no more chances for you. I am hereby sentencing you to one year in a California State Prison." His gavel falls like a guillotine.

CHAPTER 14

A LETTER FROM PRISON

C hecking our mailbox daily, we receive an unfamiliar prison-is-sued envelope addressed to our family. It's from Tommy. In the upper left-hand corner, the prison return address is typed in red print, and Tommy wrote his legal name and prison ID number underneath. Staring at every written detail, I choke back emotions. We've become familiar with Tommy's absences in our daily life, but when the revolving door through the criminal system begins to consistently repeat itself, we grieve each time. We start to learn how to turn our feelings on and off when he gets arrested. If we know that he is in our local Ventura County Jail, we can feel comforted by the thought that he will be fed, housed, and fairly safe, because we are able to visit him and see for ourselves how he is doing. But when Tommy's letter arrives from a state prison (reputedly the least safe of all the detainment centers), it is a horrific reminder that our son's life could now be in jeopardy.

I don't want to open the letter right away, feeling Tom and I should be together. Walking back from the mailbox, I wonder what our long-time mailman must think about these letters from attorneys, police, courts, and prisons. He must remember Tommy as the sweet, smiling youngster that used to run to greet him.

I open the door and announce, "We've got a letter from Tommy."

Lisa, Jeff, Ted, and Laurie happen to be visiting our house, so we all sit down at our dining room table to read the letter together. Neither

Tom nor I can bear to read his words out loud, so we pass the letter along so each person can read it for themselves.

> *"Dear Family, I am missing you all so much. I really messed up. I'm sorry my life is taking such a toll on everyone. I hate that my drug use has so affected Kim, Elijah and me...I stand out from most of the inmates here. I've been told I look like a surfer, so they call me 'Turtle' and 'Tortuga'. I like my new name because it reminds me of the ocean I am missing so much."*

I re-read his letter several times, tracing my fingers over his words written in pencil. I can't hold our son, but I can hold this letter, and that's better than nothing.

CHAPTER 15

PAROLE...AND PRISON

Tommy ends up serving only half of his prison sentence. We find out that if inmates stay out of trouble while incarcerated, they can serve what is called "half time." When we pick Tommy up at the prison release gate, his paperwork states he'll be on parole for two years. He is also given the name of his parole officer and the time and day he is to report to him.

Within a couple days of Tommy's release, the three of us are at home and well into our evening when we are startled by the sound of loud, aggressive pounding on our front door. We don't know who it could possibly be. Our property is completely fenced in with an electronic gate and can only be opened with a gate code. Tommy hesitates. Barely opening our front door to peer out, two large men pumped with adrenaline forcefully push open our door, push by Tommy, and step inside our house.

Calling out their identities, we hear "I'm Parole Agent Shyly!"

"Deputy Sheriff Belford!" Then Deputy Belford demands to know with a loud voice, "Do you keep firearms in this house?"

Tom stands up and directly answers this militant behavior with a forceful, "No!"

"We're here for Mr. Thomas Lennon, Jr. Is that you?"

Tommy nods his head yes. The agent immediately requests a urine sample to test Tommy for illegal drugs in his system. Tommy walks towards the bathroom with the agent on his heels. Deputy Belford demands that Tom show him which room Tommy is staying in. Following Tom down our hallway, the Sheriff draws a flashlight, flicks it on, and squeezes past Tom with his big belly.

Hoping to find parole violations like alcohol, drugs, drug paraphernalia, weapons, a passport, or airline tickets, he enters Tommy's room and randomly begins pulling clothes from his closet. Violently shaking each item, he then tosses it to the floor. He does the same with the chest of drawers until everything is emptied, and the carpet is no longer visible. Plowing through Tommy's desk with both arms, he shoves all the papers to the floor, including artwork that Tommy's been tirelessly working on. Then yanking bed covers and sheets off the bed, he strips the pillows of their cases expecting something to fall out from inside them.

Dropping to his stomach, the Sheriff aims his flashlight under the bed pulling out tennis shoes, flip flops, and a skateboard. In a rage at having found nothing illegal, he throws surfer magazines about the room. In frustration, they leave our home without so much as a goodbye, let alone an apology. Left to wonder how they got onto our property, Tom opens our front door and sees that our front gate is still open. He uses the gate clicker to close it, but it doesn't close.

The following morning Tom calls Tommy's parole agent, "Is this Agent Shyly? How did you get onto our property last night without a gate code? Our gate is frozen now and won't close."

"We use a key like the fire department uses in case of a fire. I'll send a deputy out to reset it."

The agent ended the phone call but accidentally didn't hang up the phone. Tom overhears the agent saying to another person, "Yeah, it's really creepy out there. It's all dark, kinda spooky."

Then Tom realizes that the agent is talking with Tommy's psychiatrist who responds with, "Yeah, that guy creeps me out, he has a weird eye." Then Tom hears a click and a dial tone.

I mean, I'm sorry, but...WTF?!? What kind of doctor breaks patient-doctor confidentiality and says such unkind, uncompassionate things about their patient?!

Living in the ongoing, hypervigilant stress of being on parole, Tommy frequently asks, "What time is it? Do I have enough time to eat? Shower? Can I start an art project today?"

He doesn't know how to relax. He tells us, "Day and night, I keep thinking...what if I screw up again and get thrown back in prison?!"

The parole system has set the bar of performance so high that it has the appearance of being designed for people like our son, Tommy, to fail. When Tommy has to take public transportation to a parole visit and the buses don't arrive on time, his parole officer adds even more stress to Tommy's structure by telling him, "If you are even one minute late, I can send you back to prison. So don't you blow it!"

Weekly parole meetings include random drug testing and turning in mandatory twelve-step meeting cards with a required signature confirming his attendance. We recall what the Twin Tower Jail doctor told Tom and I about Tommy attending twelve step meetings, "While I think highly of the twelve-step programs, if the primary issue is an undiagnosed Traumatic Brain Injury, Tommy will never hit bottom, or 'bottom out,' as it's referred to. It's not like someone who has a drug or alcohol problem."

When the judge sentenced Tommy to prison, he knew that Tommy had only been on probation, which is way less demanding than parole. Now for the next two years, under the eagle eye of a parole officer, Tommy lives with the threat of being returned to prison again and again. Had Tommy come before a judge and a public defender who were educated on Traumatic Brain Injury and its many symptoms, perhaps Tommy's behaviors and actions wouldn't have warranted such harsh sentencing.

In an effort to help Tommy's parole officer understand his limitations and how TBI impacts his behavior, Tom gets in touch with the Forensic Psychiatrist from the Twin Towers Jail and asks if he could send a letter regarding his observations and interaction with Tommy while he was incarcerated in Los Angeles. Maybe hearing it from a professional will elicit more compassion and understanding.

To whom this may concern,

This letter is written on behalf of Thomas Lennon Jr. and his parents, Mr. and Mrs. Thomas Lennon. I am a Child and Adolescent Forensic Psychiatrist presently in fellowship training at the USC Institute of Psychiatry and Law. Thomas came to my attention as part of my regular duty at the Twin Towers Jail Inmate Reception Center. He underwent a psychiatric screening evaluation that I performed as part of his intake to the jail. This letter seeks to inform the Court as to the potential presence of a serious psychiatric condition, a Traumatic Brain Injury secondary to head trauma, suffered by Thomas Lennon which, if present, could decrease his ability to control his impulses and possibly explain the series of impulsive acts. During my evaluation of Thomas, I became impressed with the combination of psychiatric symptoms he displays in association with what is reported to me as a series of recurrent and highly impulsive acts. In particular, I am impressed with Thomas' history of a severe head injury that, in my opinion, may underline much of Thomas' difficulty controlling his impulses and hence, his difficulty refraining from impulsive behavior which may cause him to break the law. At age (sixteen) Thomas, an accomplished surfer, suffered a very serious injury to his head when he was hit in the forehead by his surfboard. This resulted in a possible hairline fracture to the skull and Thomas losing consciousness while in large surf, necessitating his being rescued by a friend. It is not known if Thomas went without oxygen for a significant period while he was in the water, further increasing his risk of brain injury. More than half of the patients with moderate head trauma have ongoing neuro psychiatric symptoms resulting from head trauma. The two major types of symptoms related to head trauma are cognitive impairment and behavioral problems.

Please do not hesitate to contact me if I may be of further assistance to the Court in this matter.

-Murphy, M.D., Fellow of Forensic Psychiatry USC Institute of Psychiatry & Law

As life moves forward and away from our first confrontation with parole, no matter how much or how often we try to help him, Tommy's mental foundation continues to erode.

We are starting to accept that love and support can't fix the damaged impulse control area of Tommy's brain. And it can't heal the area of his brain that allows a normal person to remember what gets them into trouble. Instead, Tommy starts to buckle under the severity of life on such a short leash.

One day on our way to a parole visit, Tommy's knee starts bobbing up and down feverishly like a sewing machine needle. He starts taking in deep breaths, then gently exhales them. I'm so aware of what he is doing, I find myself clenching my hands around the steering wheel. Tommy starts to laugh, then nervously lets out a huge sigh and blurts, "Mom, I messed up! I was at the beach when I ran into an old friend. He offered me some marijuana, and I didn't think twice, and I smoked some!"

"Tommy, this is not–"

He interrupts me, "I knew you were going to be upset Mom, but don't worry, it was just once! But I'm gonna tell my parole officer. He's a good guy, and he knows I've been doing really good and trying really hard."

Optimism in the face of a punitive criminal system is something Tommy pulls off without much effort, but could this naive, casual attitude be caused by his brain injury? Or is it Tommy's natural innate buoyancy? Seemingly, no matter how hard the obstacle or circumstance he faces, he sees a spark of humanity in every person and thinks that his honesty can merit lenience.

Tommy is sentenced to serve time in prison for admitting his guilt and violating his parole.

After a few weeks, we receive another thick envelope with STATE PRISON GENERATED MAIL stamped in bold red letters above Tommy's name. I can feel the heaviness of where this letter comes from. I sit down in the sunshine on the front steps. A family of deer are grazing in the field together next to our house. My heart yearns for simpler times when our children were at home safely within arm's reach of our care.

I open the envelope and begin to read.

Dear family, I love you and miss you so much it makes me cry. I'm trying to hang tuff and stay physically and mentally sane. The time seems to be going by so slow...I thought I would be out for my b'day cause I know they made a movie of my life. I am totally stoked. I've been totally freed from all my worries, and since the great weight has been lifted, and I get my son Elijah back, I've been busting mad free styles like never been heard before. I feel so blessed and grateful and I can't wait to celebrate with you and pick out beats to match my raps I've been busting because I know it's all being recorded. I'm sure you already know when I'm coming home, and I can't wait to see The Tommy Lennon Project, *the story of my life.*

One week later, another letter arrives from a different prison.

I'm back at California Men's Colony. I've been to three prisons in three weeks and now I'm back here again. I have been confined to cell living the whole time, but I got out one day and saw some old friends in the yard and breakdanced. At Wasco, it was a nightmare. They strap me down for rapping too loud and give me shots. I figure it will all be in Part II of the movie. I've been held in a lock-up observation unit my whole time at CMC and it's nothin' pretty. They give me a shot every time I start rapping loud cause I get excited and think I'm going home, like every day, because the guards tell me, 'Your father is here to pick you up,' then I roll up my belongings and go to step outside of my cell and they beat me down and report that they can't open my cell door without me trying to escape.

I can't believe what I am reading. The "Prison with a Heart," as California Men's Colony is dubbed on a national television special, throws our son into isolation on the medical side of the prison.

Dear Family, they keep the fluorescent lighting and air-conditioning on 24 hours, every single day. If I don't rap or dance, I can earn a piece of clothing, one at a time, eventually I can earn a blanket.

Then another letter:

Sorry so sloppy, it's because I'm in (isolation) right now, and they give you this floppy pencil so you can't hurt yourself or shank somebody else with it. But it's not so bad cause I've already made friends through my music. It's like no matter where I go, I always find people that I know. Even when I'm out of Ventura, now everybody knows me and it feels great with all the vibes I get...I guess I got me a beach house at Pitus Point that is off the hook! This is so unbelievable that this is happening to our family. We're all blowin' up! I know I had to go through a lot of pain and heartache to make this possible, but it makes me feel so good that you guys are so proud of me and love me

*unconditionally the way you do. And that's a rap. No
need to say I love you. Forever and eternity,*

XOXOXOXO

We cannot comprehend what is happening to him. No matter how
many times Tommy asks for visiting forms, he is denied. Why isn't he
allowed visitors? Why is he being transferred from prison to prison to
prison? Forced injections? What medicine are they injecting him with?
We have no idea what this is all about. With so many questions we can
only wait for Tommy's next letter and make up scenarios in our minds
to fill in the blanks.

Tom and I cope with this unbearable sense of helplessness and
grief by attending twelve-step Al Anon meetings and going to therapy.
Holding on to each other through the tempest of our lives, we fall into
a restless sleep night after night. We begin a daily routine of walking,
prayer, and meditation to get through this unthinkable dilemma. Day
after day, continuing to do these practices, we begin to feel like we
are moving more calmly and thinking more clearly, and that's when
Tommy's next letter arrives:

Dear family,

*I still don't have a release date yet and I have not been
able to go outside for 2 1/2 months. I've been locked down.
Say a prayer for me that I'm able to go outside soon. I
hate being hungry in here. I miss everyone so much and it
makes me sad I didn't see Elijah this summer, but when
I get out, I get him forever. The worst that can happen*

is I stay in here til Jan. 29th. They are trying to max me out (the maximum sentence time possible). I got into some trouble when I was rapping loud, and I wouldn't cuff up to get a shot cause I was sick of shots, so 4 officers came in and beat me down and gave me a shot and the prison court's judge gave me 150 more days to serve. Oh well, life goes on and I've turned my cell into a dojo and I'm in good shape. I did 300 crunches the other day and I have no mercy on my body. I figure I'll just take out my frustrations and sweat, blood and tears and "benefit" from this time mentally cause it mentally feels good. You wanted me to describe what the hole is like?

Well, I'm inside my cell all the time. My cell is as wide as my arms stretch out. I can take six steps from the door to the toilet. I have a window that I can open or shut, but I cannot really see that good out of it cause it's made up of tiny steel holes and bars. On certain days, I am asked if I want to shower, in which case, I handcuff up and step out backwards to be escorted to the shower. Once I'm in the shower, they take the handcuffs off. On Tuesdays I get a squirt of shampoo. The other times I can leave my cell is to see the psych once a week or to go to the so-called yard. The yard is a small enclosed room I go to by myself with a handball inside. They give me a t-shirt, socks and boxers when I shower and that is usually what I wear in my cell. But they also give you a white jumpsuit and flip flops when you first come to the hole. This jumpsuit you wear when you go to see the doctor or lawyer or such. When I go to the doctor, I am handcuffed and escorted across the yard to his office, so once a week I do get to see outside. They bring a book cart around once a week, and you can pick out two books. Back to my cell, I have a desk and four shelves, a sink and a toilet and a light switch. Well that pretty much wraps up my life in the hole.

Love, Tommy

Tommy's letters now arrive regularly and often. As many as three letters get delivered to our mailbox in one day. In more detail he writes:

...satellites are filming my every move, people all over the world can see what they are doing to me on their computer screens. I know this is happening to me so they'll stop building jails and prisons. I believe I'm suffering to set the prisoners free and that on my birthday, Kim and Elijah and I will be a family again, and there will no longer be money, and I'll get to see the movie of my life.

Reading this letter to our therapist, she recognizes that this behavior pattern is what has been described as "a special strategy that a person invents in order to live in an unlivable situation."

After five months of getting letters from Tommy about the abuse and isolation, our daughter Lisa telephones us and reports, "I am watching a primetime television special and what Tommy's going through is illegal."

By 8:00 a.m. the next morning I am on the telephone with Tommy's parole officer.

"Agent Shyly, this is Debbie Lennon. Our son Tommy has been in isolation for five months, and his mental condition is deteriorating. The prison won't give Tommy visitation forms so we are unable to see him. We've been informed that what's happening to our son is illegal."

Shyly takes a deep breath and pauses. When he finally speaks, he says, "Tommy should have never been sent to prison in the first place. Whatever Tommy's done in the past, it never warranted prison time."

I can barely speak. Trying to gain the strength to repeat what was just said to me, I question, "Tommy should have never been sent to prison???"

I heard nothing on the other end of the telephone. Sitting in silence I trust Shyly is still on the line. Clearing his throat he asks me, "Have you got a pen or pencil? The number I'm giving you is a direct line to Tommy's treating psychiatrist at California Men's Colony Prison. Tell him everything you just told me."

CHAPTER 16

HOW CAN WE FIX THIS?

I feel like my heart could explode with rage, but it's not stopping me. In fact, it has kindled a brand new fire inside me to keep knocking until someone opens the door and helps Tommy. Hanging up the telephone, I call the treating psychiatrist at the prison and leave a message. By the end of the day, I call again and leave the same message.

"This is Deborah Lennon. I am the mother of Thomas Patrick Lennon Jr. It's been brought to our attention that what is happening to our son, who has been in isolation for five months, is unlawful. To further discuss this, please call."

After several weeks of repetitive messages, our telephone rings. I hear a man's voice ask me, "Is this Mrs. Lennon, Thomas Patrick Lennon Jr.'s mother?"

"Yes?"

"I'm your son Thomas' treating psychiatrist at California Men's Colony." Then there's a long pause. "I've heard all of your messages. Did you think I wouldn't get back to you?"

I thought a callback from this doctor would validate every second of advocacy it has taken to be heard, but the voice on the other end of the phone sounds cold and smug.

"Doctor, we have been denied visitation for five months. Our son writes to us saying we cannot see him as long as he's in isolation. The first two and a half months, he said he was in an observation cell on the medical side of the prison. Then from medical observation he was thrown into the hole for another two and a half months because prison guards said he attacked them."

There is no response on the other end, but I can hear him shuffling through papers.

"The letters he's writing are of grave concern to us. He writes about how lonely he is, and that he thinks satellites are filming him so that people will see how he's suffering. He says when this information gets out, it will set the prisoners free, and there will be no more jails, prisons or money, and that's why this is happening to him."

When I tell the doctor about the television show that revealed situations like our son's, and that they are against the law, the doctor finally speaks.

"The only way your son can get out of the hole and back into a unit where you can visit him is with a new release date."

I am puzzled. "A new release date? Is that why Tommy keeps writing to us saying he still doesn't know when he's getting out of prison? Because he doesn't have a release date?"

"Yes. Because of his assault on prison guards, he was given more time to serve, and he doesn't have a release date."

"What would have happened to Tommy if I hadn't called?"

"Well, eventually his prison sentence would have run out, and he'd be released from this institution."

My heart is pounding inside my head like a thunderous tsunami about to hit the coastline. When I finally speak, I can barely get the words out, "And why has no one put him on the calendar for a new release date, so that he can get out of isolation and have visitors?"

"I can do that, and I will do that."

As I am saying thank you, he's already hung up the telephone. Feeling hopeful and in disbelief simultaneously, I melt into the nearest chair and break down sobbing from the effects of our conversation.

Calling my therapist is the only thing I feel capable of doing. I tell her about how deeply affected I am after dealing with someone in the criminal system, and how some people's work ethics seem so unlawful and senseless to me. To help me better understand what our family is going through, she takes the time to read from a current article she saved.

"'Destabilization is caused by living under secondary incarceration, by proximity through a loved one.' That is what's happening to you and your family."

She's right. What's happening in our communities, right under our noses, is not only affecting our family, but tens of thousands of families just like ours all throughout the United States of America. How is it possible that all of us with loved ones who are brain injured, or mentally ill, or both, are getting steamrolled over by the atrocities, corruption, and negligent behaviors within our criminal system?

Before Tommy can get released from the hole and put into the general population of the prison where we can visit him, he appears before a judge. Not only is he given a new release date, but his psychiatrist writes a mandatory, court-approved prescription for a bipolar disorder medication.

Every morning and every night, Tommy lines up to take behavioral medication. A guard who dispenses pharmacy prescriptions to the prisoners happens to have grown up in our neighborhood with Tommy, and Tommy recognizes him. Then he recognizes Tommy. They both know not to acknowledge one another, or they could get into trouble.

That same day, I receive an unexpected telephone call.

"Mrs. Lennon, this is Rusty Brooks, your old neighbor. I just saw Tommy at the Men's Colony. I'm a guard here." Rusty's voice sounds small and quiet, like he's whispering so that he cannot be overheard. "I dispense medication, and Tommy was in my line. I had to call you! What's a guy like Tommy doing in prison? Tommy's one of the nicest guys I've ever known in my life!"

After telling Rusty a synopsis of Tommy's story, he says, "Yeah, bad stuff goes down here all of the time, Mrs. Lennon. I'm so sorry."

Two weeks after being put on medication, we receive visiting applications from Tommy. Filling them out, and mailing them back to the prison on the same day, another two weeks pass before we finally get the approval we need to see our son.

On the morning of our assigned visiting day, we wake up earlier than usual in the anticipation of the unknown. Having packed our essentials the night before, we leave early, drive a couple hours north and take the highway that goes through the seaside town of San Luis Obispo. On the fringe of the city, we pass the California Men's Colony on our right and continue north to the small coastal town of Cambria, where we have our motel reservations. Over the years Tom and I often vacation in Cambria because it's so close to our home and such a great getaway. But now under extremely heartbreaking circumstances, we can only hope *our* Cambria will comfort us.

Within an hour of arriving and getting settled into our room, we are back in our vehicle and driving along the coast towards the prison. Turning into the parking lot, the facility looks overwhelmingly bleak. Razor-edged, steel barbed wire is prominent along the tops of the gates and the perimeter of the fencing. What seems to stretch for miles into the distance looks like an impenetrable fortress. A guard stands in a tower at the entrance silhouetted against a dark looming sky. He positions his rifle so that it is visible. Tom parks our truck, and we walk toward the facility. Just picking up our feet takes effort, as though we are pushing through dense mud with every step towards the prison.

When we arrive at the reception station, we are instructed to stop at a podium. A woman in a prison issued police uniform tells us, "You need to fill out information cards." The prison requires the name of who we are visiting, the booking number, and our relationship to the prisoner. Having read the visiting guidelines before arriving at the prison, we provide a picture identification card, but leave everything else inside our vehicle including my purse, Tom's wallet, and any extra clothing besides the jackets we are wearing. Change is allowed inside the prison for the vending machines, but it must be put inside a clear plastic baggie, which we have with us.

Asking us to hand over our vehicle keys we are told, "Take your shoes and your belts off. The contents of your pockets need to be emptied out, and placed into this plastic tray."

After being instructed to walk through metal detectors, we pull ourselves back together and are told, "Pull up your right sleeve, and expose the inside of your wrist." We get stamped with a neon yellow colored ink, which will be checked under a black light when we leave the facility. The robotic protocols and lack of sensitivity is chilling. Feeling as though we are being treated like criminals, we find that not one person is cordial.

Finally being handed the visiting pass we had been waiting on for six months, I can only compare it to that young boy Charlie from *Willy Wonka & the Chocolate Factory*. Unwrapping his candy bar, he discovers he's won the last Golden Ticket. We, too, have won something extraordinarily precious; this slip of paper is going to let us see our boy today.

We follow a guard through different areas of the prison, and a deafening buzzer sounds every time a metal gate or sliding door electronically opens. After we walk through each entryway, the doors slam shut with such force, it feels like they'll never open again. There is a mild metallic odor that reminds me of the old-fashioned filling materials dentists used in my childhood. At a high wooden countertop, we hand our golden ticket to one of three guards working inside a large metal cage. The guard takes that slip of paper with Tommy's name on it and uses their in-house telephone to summon him to the visiting area. While being handed written instructions on the rules of physical greetings, we are told to wait at a circular white Formica table.

Visitors push chairs from one table to another to accommodate different sized groups. The stark white enamel painted surfaces, the cement floors, and the frigid, air-conditioned temperatures seem more like a morgue than a "prison with a heart."

Tom and I watch as one inmate at a time enters the room. Walking over to the cage, they hand in their visiting slip to a guard. Then they return to where they had entered the room and stand behind a red line on the floor. Taking a wide stance, they spread their legs apart and place their hands behind their backs. This cues visitors that they can be approached. The watchful eyes of a guard monitor how long loved ones can hug and even how they kiss.

It seems like we are waiting a really long time when Tommy finally pops through the door into the brightly lit room. Quickly delivering his slip of paper to the cage, he walks back to the red line and waits for our embrace. Tom and I can't get to him fast enough! Tom puts his arms around us all just like when Tommy was first born. Hanging onto one another, we can't let go. Non-stop tears flow like rivers down all of our faces. I need to let the moment penetrate my senses. I need to remember this feeling of hugging our son and the steady rise and fall of his breathing under my hand.

Settling into our visit, food aromas fill the air. People use microwave ovens to cook popcorn and heat burritos. We ask Tommy if he wants anything from the vending machines.

He says, "You'll have to walk over there with me because prisoners are not allowed to handle money or touch the vending machines and microwaves." Tommy gets a burrito, some peanut M&M's, and a root beer.

Less than an hour into our visit, he starts talking about the same delusion he wrote about in his letters.

"I know everyone can see what they're doing to me. You and Dad, everyone can see me on their computers." He pauses and pours some M&Ms into his mouth looking back and forth at us. "I don't know why you act like you don't know what I'm talking about. You guys know the satellites filmed me rapping and dancing in the hole because you watched it on your computer, and now I'm famous, and they're making a movie about my life! Why else would they have done this to me?" Answering his own question, he says, "People have to know what's happening in here so that the prisoners can be set free, of course!"

Tom and I exchange concerned glances.

"Tommy, we don't know anything about filming," Tom says quietly. "I know you've been through a lot..."

"Yes!!! You do know I've been through a lot because you've been watching me on your computer! Just stop lying!!!! Why are you lying?!!!!!" Tommy's jaw clenches tightly around his words. Then he slams his hands on the table and stands up, threatening to overturn the table. I frantically scan the room looking for the guards to see if they are picking up on the heightened activity at our table. Tom uses an old trick from parenting younger children and quickly puts his hand on Tommy's while changing the subject.

"Have you been getting your commissary money for extra food and postage stamps?"

It's the right question.

Sitting back down at the table, he switches tracks immediately and answers with gratitude. As long as we don't challenge his new beliefs, our visit continues to go smoothly. We stay with him until we hear an announcement over the PA system, "Visiting time is over, clear the area."

We confirm with Tommy, "We'll be returning tomorrow to spend more time with you."

We walk towards the painted red line on the floor and take our positions. With Tom and I on one side of the line, Tommy is with a guard on the other side. Tommy leans in over the line to hug me. The thought of leaving him there feels like an unforgivable betrayal. I burrow a kiss into his cheek, in the hopes of imprinting the memory forever. Overriding all our years of protective parenting instincts, we are forced to walk away from our son.

As we exit the visiting area, a guard leads us through the same security gates. We put our wrists under a black light for security clearance. A guard hands us our vehicle keys. In silence, we walk back to the truck. Behind us we can still hear the unrelenting echoes of heavy metal doors slamming shut with such permanence and certainty.

Leaving Tommy at the mercy of the California Men's Colony staff and its guards, I begin to wonder, what are the qualifications needed to work in a prison? How can the responsibility of protecting damaged lives like our son's be given to prison guards wearing clubbing batons, tasers, and guns?

Tears streaming from our eyes and a pelting rain makes it almost impossible to see the lines on the road. In all our years of parenting, we have been through many difficulties, but we can't even begin to comprehend what we have just experienced. In shock and disbelief, our silence lasts the entire drive back to our motel room.

Getting settled into our evening, the only thought we exchange is, *how can we fix this?* We agree to call our family therapist and tell her about our visit with Tommy.

She surmises, "It sounds as if Tommy has had a psychotic break."

"What does that mean?"

"It means he's living in another reality, something he can make sense of."

When I ask her how long it can last, she says, "I don't know. Some come back quicker than others. Some don't come back at all."

CHAPTER 17

GOOD PEOPLE TRY TO HELP

A fter our visits with Tommy, we attend an Al-Anon meeting. A small woman with kind, sparkling eyes approaches us and introduces herself.

"Hi, I'm Robbie. I've been listening to your stories for months now. Have you ever heard of a group called NAMI? The National Alliance for the Mentally Ill? NAMI's mission is to break the silence and stigma associated with mental illness, to return dignity to the person who is ill, and to their families as well. There's a meeting tonight if you're interested?"

Driving into Ventura later that day, we find the church grounds and the building where the NAMI meetings are held. Inside, folks are already seated at a large round table in the kitchen of the facility. As this pre-meeting gets called to order, I look around the table to see what mentally ill people's families look like. The illness doesn't discriminate. It touches all races, income levels, and religions. Mothers, fathers, sisters, brothers, aunts, uncles, grandparents, and friends all gather around this table to tell their stories.

One grandmother shares, "Some days are good and somehow we've accumulated a few good weeks."

Then a young mother says, "It's almost impossible for me on my own to proceed in a daily routine. I've got to take my younger child to daycare before I go to work. When my older daughter is in a mental health crisis, I am unable to do that. I watch her cycle through the mania from bi-polar disorder. There are so many stages to get through. When she finally stabilizes, it feels like it's gone on forever. My husband divorced me a year ago. My family and friends have all fallen away. I don't blame them. I'm in a crisis so often, there's no consistency in our lives whatsoever."

So many different kinds of experiences are shared, but the common thread that runs through all of our lives is the devastation of living with mental illness.

The general meeting is held in a much larger room. Rows of folding chairs are set up facing a podium, and at the back of the room, banquet tables are filled with NAMI literature, coffee, tea, and dessert. We hear updates from the president, the secretary, the treasurer, and then their representative for legislation. My mind goes from a heap of confusion into some semblance of order as each representative speaks efficiently and effectively. Their efforts are towards making a difference by educating and enriching people's lives.

An attractive woman steps up to the microphone and shares, "Hi! I'm Sonia. We have a new starting date for the Family-to-Family classes. We meet once a week for two hours. The course lasts six weeks. We'll learn about what our loved ones go through when hearing voices. We will learn how to create a calm space for a client when in crisis. I will be teaching how we can't allow our fear to escalate their fear, which can turn into chaos and must be dealt with appropriately without anyone getting hurt."

The class sounds like an incredible, life-changing opportunity for Tom and me. We look at one another and, without exchanging words, nod our heads in agreement that we want to sign up for the class.

Sonia goes on to say, "Next on our agenda, please welcome Officer Mark Stadler and his boss Lieutenant Thurston from the Ventura

County Police Department. They have a new mental health program they would like to introduce to us, so let's give them a round of applause."

After brief introductions, Officer Mark Stadler shares a true story about when he was a rookie in the Ventura Police Department.

"When I was new in the department, I responded to a call with an experienced officer I had never met before. The call was an assault with a deadly weapon in progress, and I later learned the man involved was suffering a mental health crisis. The experienced officer arrived on scene first and attempted to talk to the subject who was non-responsvie after attacking two people with a machete. When I arrived, the experienced officer decided that we would spray the armed subject with a chemical spray to get him to surrender. After warning him and then spraying, the subject charged toward me swinging the machete. Because our lives were in danger, I fired my gun."

Mark pauses and covers both his eyes with one hand. He's pushing in on his eyes with his fingers trying to block the tears. It takes courage to share this story with a room full of people who love someone just like that mentally ill man. After gathering his composure, Mark's voice falls to a lower pitch.

"I killed him. I took his life." His words fell hard on all of us. "That didn't need to happen, but I didn't know that at the time."

Mark pauses again and clears his throat before continuing. "After taking some time off from my job, I knew that law enforcement needed to make a change, a difference. I attended a training course called Crisis Intervention Training, or CIT, and immediately knew this was the answer I had been looking for. CIT teaches law enforcement how to de-escalate potentially dangerous situations with persons suffering from a mental illness. Working with other law enforcement agencies, the National Alliance on Mental Illness, and Ventura County Behavioral Health, we built our own CIT program in Ventura County. So if your loved one is ever in crisis, please ask the 9-1-1 operator for a CIT trained officer."

After the meeting, we introduce ourselves and thank Mark for his courage to change things after such a tragic event. He asks me if I would be interested in speaking on behalf of our son's condition at one of his CIT courses. I agree wholeheartedly and feel included and committed to making a difference in any way I can.

Walking out to our car, I think about all our years in Al-Anon and learning about "tough love." Al-Anon is an extremely helpful concept for someone who loves an alcoholic or an addict. However, in our case, tough love is apparently not the answer. Is there an answer for dealing with a brain injured loved one?

CHAPTER 18

RELEASED

Tommy is scheduled to get out of prison at the end of the month. At thirty-two years old and having served two years on parole, there will be no more reporting to his parole officer or random drug testing. As they say in the criminal world, "He ran out his parole."

On this cold January day, we will drive to the prison to pick Tommy up. As we enter the perimeters of the prison I look up, and the guard in the tower is again holding his rifle, so that it is readily apparent he has a weapon. I have trouble believing I am in America.

Entering the reception area, Tom and I are practically running to the desk. I cannot wait to hug Tommy again. The receiving officer starts the usual check in process, but I interrupt her and say, "Oh no, we are not visiting today. Our son is being released, and we're here to pick him up!"

We are still asked to fill out an information card, as if we were visiting Tommy inside the prison. Waiting for our son to get processed and released doesn't hurt like it did when we knew we had to say goodbye and leave him there. Walking through those blackened steel bars for the last time, we see Tommy's bright smile, and we can tangibly feel his exuberance. After a quick hug, he's skipping three stairs at a time, sliding down the handrail, doing laps around us all the way out to the parking lot, while joyfully proclaiming again and again "I am a free man! I'm free, I'm free!"

When we ask him about the medication they had ordered him to take before being released from solitary, he quips, "Oh I stopped taking that two weeks ago!"

"Why?"

"Because they asked me if I wanted to go off of my medication, and I said yes!"

Once we get home, I immediately call the prison psychiatrist, and it's a miracle he picks up my call. "This is Thomas Patrick Lennon Jr's mother. Our son Thomas was released today from the prison. Why wasn't he sent home with medication or a prescription for medication?"

"Prisoners have rights too!" The psychiatrist indignantly replied, as if I should know that. He further informs me, "Two weeks prior to a prisoner's release, they can choose to go off their medications if they want to, and your son chose to go off of his. But you know what? By the way he was behaving in here after going off of his medication, we'll be seeing him again soon. He'll be back here in no time at all."

Sickened by what the doctor just said, I can't believe what I am hearing. The California Men's Colony, with their barbaric system, reduces our son's ability to think and act independently by what appears to us to be torturing him and guaranteeing that the *for-profit* criminal system will soon have a return customer. *We'll be seeing him again soon.* Tommy, never of criminal mind or intent, thinks of himself as a free man. But in reality, he is now serving a life sentence of delusional thinking, post-traumatic stress disorder, anxieties, and unwanted voices inside his head.

The day after Tommy's release, Tom and I know that we need to get Tommy psychiatric support immediately. On our way to the clinic to enroll him in outpatient mental health services, we stop at a red light.

Suddenly, with the quick movements of a feral cat, Tommy climbs out the small back window of our truck and jumps into our empty truck bed. Then jumping out of that, and onto the street, he starts jogging towards the beach. Looking back over his shoulder, and running as fast as he can, he's waving goodbye with a huge grin on his face reminiscent of the nursery rhyme, "Catch me if you can, I'm the gingerbread man."

Recalling Tommy's prison letters, a frightening thought crosses our minds. What if he's on his way to find the beach house he wrote about in his delusional letters? The one he thinks he owns? What if he enters someone's home and frightens them? Or even gets shot?

Calling 911 and identifying myself, I ask if a CIT officer can help us. I explain to the dispatcher that our son is heading towards the beach, and that he believes he owns a beach house down near Pitus Point. The dispatcher asks for our exact location and tells us she'll send a CIT trained officer out to assist as soon as possible.

Following Tommy as far as we can drive, we pull our truck over and park in a dirt lot near the beach. After walking a bit, we spot Tommy with two officers. Luckily, they are the CIT trained police. As we approach them, we observe that they are staying very calm and allowing a lot of space between themselves and Tommy. Tom and I stop a short distance away. Tommy can see us, but we don't want to interrupt. We can hear Tommy defending himself.

"I haven't done anything wrong! Nothing unlawful!"

After the officers talk with him for a while, they assess that Tommy is delusional. One of the officers takes out his handcuffs, causing the situation to quickly escalate into a struggle. As Tommy twists his body to try and get away, the officer calmly detains him and brings him to the ground.

Tommy cries out in confusion and disbelief. "Dad!!!! What have I done?! Why is this happening?!"

Tom could barely utter the words he was about to say to our son. "Tommy, you need help."

As one officer is putting Tommy in the back of their patrol car, the other one gives Tom and I directions to the acute psychiatric hospital in Ventura. "It's called Hillmont, and it's next to the Ventura County Hospital."

Walking back to our truck, we see Tommy pass by in the backseat of the police car. Tom and I feel completely destroyed by what just occurred. I wonder out loud, "Is this the only illness where a person in need of medical attention gets handcuffed and taken to a hospital in the backseat of a police car?"

We arrive at the hospital and park, then ascend cement steps to the entrance. Tom tries to open the glass entry door, but it's locked. Pushing a small black button on a speaker box mounted next to the door we hear, "How can I help you?"

Tom starts to explain our situation, but he's interrupted.

"Please come inside."

A startling, loud buzzing sound, much like at the prison, unlocks the front door. The reception area is well-lit and spacious. A low-grade hum from fluorescent lighting and a noisy ventilation system seem to absorb all the sound, like being under water. The receptionist tells us, "Your son is in intake. Go right through those doors."

We push through the doors and see Tommy halfway down the hallway with his back to us. The doctor is trying to evaluate Tommy, but Tommy is too upset to cooperate.

The doctor sees us approaching and demands, "Stop! Don't enter!"

Several hospital aides rush past us with restraints and descend all over Tommy. Tommy is yelling as loudly as he can, "Dad please! Help me, Dad! What have I done?! Please!! Make this all stop!"

We stay in the hallway so as not to interfere, but we can still see everything that is happening to our son. So deeply conflicted as I watch my son struggling, I ask myself if calling the police was the best choice. But what alternative did we have? The treating psychiatrist takes out a single syringe while a male attendant pulls at Tommy's clothing, exposing Tommy's hip. The doctor administers a shot, and within seconds Tommy's speech begins to slur, and the twisted features on his angry, confused face melt away. He instantly falls into an induced sleep. The doctor steps out into the hallway to speak with us.

"I gave him a hefty dose of medication to sedate him, so he'll be asleep for hours. We are going to keep your son here on a 5150."

"What is that?" We both ask in unison.

"It's up to a seventy-two-hour hold. Legally, we can detain him for that amount of time to diagnose him, and come up with a recommended treatment plan."

Hearing that the doctor will recommend a treatment plan that would benefit Tommy, I feel relieved but can no longer contain my emotions. Finding the nearest chair, I sit down, cover my face with both hands, and begin to cry...like maybe I would never stop. Out of concern, Tom rests his hand on my shoulder. Looking up at Tom, he appears older, pale and just gutted.

The doctor hands me a Kleenex and asks if we want a cup of water. He then genuinely asks us, "Are you two ok?"

"We just picked Tommy up from prison yesterday, and we thought the worst was behind us," I tell him. "Within twenty-four hours, here we are leaving our firstborn son, our miracle child, at a lockdown mental hospital in the city of Ventura. The prison released a beautiful man whose life they had shattered into a million pieces. How do we even begin to try and make sense of what's happened to him?"

Tommy later signs a consent form so that Tom and I can talk with his doctors and his social worker. Visiting Tommy at the acute care hospital as often as possible, the main psychiatrist on our son's case tells us, "Thomas needs to be conserved."

Never hearing that terminology before we ask, "What does that mean?"

"It's a court-ordered legal status that appoints a person or entity to manage an incompetent individual's affairs. For young people like your son, the legal status of conservatorship lasts one calendar year, but he can contest the conservatorship every six months.

"The county's Public Guardian Office or a family member can be assigned as his conservator, who is then responsible for all his health decisions. Conservatorship would also include overseeing medications and the monthly distribution of his SSI, or his Supplemental Security Income money. That would be for housing, food, clothing, hygiene products, and any legal obligations. Only one person can legally become a conservator. Do you know which one of you would want to take on that legal title?"

Tom and I look at each other, and without words Tom points to himself.

"Yes, I will take that role on. I will be our son's conservator."

The last step to finalize the conservatorship is for a judge to hear Tommy's case in a conservatorship court, which is held in the conference room at the hospital. A public defender is appointed to ensure Tommy's civil rights are being protected. His psychiatrist is present, as is the judge, Tommy's social worker, a court recorder, and a hospital recorder. One by one, each professional takes a turn speaking. At the close of the hearing, Tommy's legal counsel informs Tommy, "You can contest your conservatorship in six months." With that final piece of information, the judge sounds his gavel. Tommy is legally conserved for one year and is free to leave the hospital and return home with us.

CHAPTER 19

CONSERVATORSHIP

T reading in uncharted waters with the conservatorship documents as our only floating device, the course of events that are taking place since Tommy's prison release redefine us all. We don't know what we are dealing with exactly, but we feel hopeful that with the new legal support, we can help steer Tommy's life in a more positive direction without him slipping through the cracks in our criminal and mental health systems.

As Tommy's conservator, the first thing Tom does is send a request to the California Men's Colony Prison for a copy of Tommy's medical records. He sends the request along with a copy of Tommy's legal conservatorship document. It is absolutely necessary that we fill in all of the blanks as to what went wrong while Tommy was locked up in isolation. Tom sends the request by certified mail and hangs on to the receipt just in case verification is ever needed.

On several occasions I telephone the prison asking them to mail Tommy's medical records to his conservator, Tom Lennon. But every time I speak with someone, they say it's a process and that it could take a long time. At this point, we wonder if we will ever receive his records.

Back at home with Tommy under our roof, we deal with one crisis after another, almost daily. His delusional talk becomes more frequent, and he repeats stories about the satellites filming him in prison.

He repeatedly talks about his birthday, the day when he, Kim, and Elijah will all become a family again.

Meanwhile our therapist explains to us that Tommy's delusions are his reality and that we should not challenge them. "What would it feel like if someone challenged *your* reality?"

While under conservatorship we manage to steer Tommy's meltdowns towards the hospital instead of incarceration. Officer Mark Stadler's newly implemented CIT lifeline to mental health services is an empowering tool for families like ours.

Mark, so deeply affected by the repetitiveness of Tommy's crises, gives us his private cell phone number and says, "Call me whenever you need help with Tommy." We call him often.

Our new reality is that every few weeks the police show up with their handcuffs and a patrol car ready to drive Tommy to the hospital. It's always a traumatizing event for Tommy, the CIT police, and us, because it's always against his will.

Institutional confinement had become so unbearable for Tommy that on one occasion, when he was taken to the psychiatric hospital in a crisis, a hospital attendant witnessed Tommy scaling over a seemingly insurmountable wall, leaving the hospital behind.

About three hours later the hospital called to tell us, "Tommy has been returned to the hospital. The police found him taking a swim in the ocean in his boxers. He appeared to be having fun, and when they apprehended him, he cooperated and appeared as happy as a clam!"

When we go to visit Tommy, he tells us about scaling the unscalable wall, "Yeah, I just pretended I was Spider Man, and I did it!"

Once Tommy initiates a thought, he can't stop himself from following through with it, until it's been done. The insanely repetitive behavior of his undiagnosed TBI makes us wonder about the onset of a condition called 'perseveration'. Perseveration is becoming fixated on a thought until it becomes an action. Sometimes perseveration can be positive, like creating art, exercising, or trying to save money and buy a bicycle. But scaling an insurmountable wall and other compulsive behaviors undermine Tommy's progress. We are learning that the damage to the impulse control area of his brain makes it harder to pause and consider the consequences of his behavior. His damaged prefrontal cortex area is no longer available to assist him in making healthy, every day, in the moment decisions.

A few days after Tommy is released from the hospital, his youngest brother Ted sees him walking towards an outbuilding on our property, carrying a thick rope in his hands.

"Dad! I just saw Tommy walking out to the cold house with a rope! It didn't look good!"

Tom rushes over to the outbuilding and interrupts Tommy, "What are you doing?"

Tommy's eyes look wild and scared, like an animal that has been cornered. "Dad!! I need the insanity to stop," he cries, slumping onto the staircase.

With another crisis on our hands, I quickly call Mark and explain to him, "Tommy's suicidal. He needs help."

Mark summons two CIT police officers to our house to take Tommy back to the Hillmont Psychiatric Hospital in Ventura. Within an hour of Tommy getting picked up at our house, we get a call from Mark.

"The hospital is refusing service to Tommy. What do you want us to do now?"

I ask him, "Do I have time to make a telephone call and get right back to you?"

I immediately call the hospital, and they tell me, "The head of Hillmont has instructed the hospital staff to decline emergency hospitalization for Tommy Lennon. Tommy apparently doesn't cooperate to our satisfaction in the outpatient treatment program and since there are people that are willing to comply, we consider Tommy a waste of our time and a waste of a bed."

Explaining that this visit is a matter of life and death, I plead for them to reconsider.

They then respond, "Tommy's needs are too chronic, acute, and critical. Tommy needs to be treated in a long-term psychiatric lockdown facility. There's a facility out in Sylmar about an hour and a half away. It could be available to him if we admit your son, and then the doctors recommend long term treatment care at Sylmar."

Grasping at this possibility, I call Mark back and tell him, "The only way Hillmont will accept Tommy is if we agree to him going into a long-term care facility, and we have."

Mark pauses and takes a breath. "I'll instruct the CIT officers to take Tommy back into Hillmont Hospital, where they can start the process for his long-term care."

Hearing great compassion in his voice, I thank Mark for every time he has responded to us in a crisis.

Visiting Tommy at Hillmont, Tom explains to Tommy, "You need time to get better after all that you have been through. Since Hillmont isn't a long-term care facility, you are going to be transferred to a long-term lockdown hospital about an hour and a half from here." Overcome with emotion, Tommy burst into tears, covering his face with both hands. The thought of being locked up again and separated from family is too much.

"How long do I have to be there, Dad?"

"We're told a year."

"Dad, nooooo, you're my conservator! Please don't let them keep me there that long. I'll work as hard as I can every day and will help when I can. But please let it only be for six months."

Tom keeps his voice very calm even when he says, "I don't think I should be the one to determine the length of time you need."

"But you're my conservator! You have complete say over my health care decisions. Can you please give me the six months I'm asking for?!"

Hesitating for a moment, I can see Tommy's mind shifting gears, and he comes back like a roaring lion, "Or I won't go there at all!!! And I'll contest my conservatorship in a couple months and be set free to do whatever I want! I know the judge will see that I'm being completely reasonable."

In that moment Tommy has great clarity and holds the winning hand. When Tommy is in a routine for *any* length of time–eating regular meals, getting rest, showering, taking medication to address the psychotic break, and being around positive, productive people that have his best interest at heart–his logic and self-awareness becomes remarkably convincing. We know he can win a judge over and no longer have to be conserved. For the sake of getting Tommy stabilized, we concede and give Tommy our word that he will only be at Sylmar Hospital for six months.

CHAPTER 20

SHINING A LIGHT ON A BROKEN SYSTEM

Sixteen years since Tommy's surf accident, and Tom and I attend a family wedding. Any Lennon wedding is basically like a huge family reunion, with dozens and dozens and dozens of Lennon's all in one place, all at one time. At the reception we see Tommy's closest cousin, Tyler, who I babysat for when he was an infant. Tyler knows about some of Tommy's recent problems and asks, "How is Tommy doing?"

"Not good, Tyler."

We fill him in on Tommy's sad and horrific story.

Tyler, who has been close with Tommy his whole life, suddenly looks pale. With tears welling in his eyes, Tyler informs me, "Aunt Debbie, you have to call my mom, she's been making documentary films, and I know she'd want to talk with you."

Feeling his love, support, and sincerity, I don't know how to respond.

"I won't tell my mom we talked. I'll leave it up to you and Uncle Tom."

About a month after the wedding, I still hadn't called my sister-in-law, Marilyn, about a documentary, but we thought about it or talked about it every day. Tom and I were trying to sort things out. Since Tommy had been suffering from the delusion that he was being filmed in prison, we were apprehensive about allowing filming to happen. Against this, we were weighing the benefit of bringing Tommy's story to the public and shining a light on the medical, legal and social issues caused by Traumatic Brain Injuries.

With trepidation, Tom and I make the decision to call Marilyn. Surprised to hear from me, and after our hello's, Marilyn gets right to the point.

"Debbie, what's going on?"

I give her a synopsis of Tommy's life up until now. She sits in complete silence, as if waiting for the happy ending that doesn't come.

"Debbie, I'm shocked," Marilyn says in a hushed tone. "I had no idea."

Her voice trails off, and memories of our boys' lives together surface in the silence. Tyler and Tommy, being the best of cousins, would spend spring break, summer vacation, and winter break together year after year. When Marilyn, a well-known print model, chose to step behind the camera lens to become a professional photographer, she asked Tommy, who was in his late teens, to be one of her models for her working portfolio. He was a natural in front of the camera, and when Marilyn submitted her work, she received an inquiry from a well-known modeling agency asking about the "blonde Elvis Presley pouty model."

"Debbie, I don't know what to say."

Did she say that to interrupt the daunting stillness on the other end of the line?

"Marilyn, we have been living this nightmare with Tommy for so long...I didn't realize how shocking this must be for you to hear all of these stories in one conversation."

When Marilyn finally speaks, she says, "I'm so sorry, Debbie. What can I do?"

"Marilyn, I've been thinking about calling you for over a month, ever since I saw Tyler at Annie's wedding. He updated me and said that you are doing documentaries. He thought that I should call you."

"Debbie! There's no way I can walk away from Tommy and his story!"

As raw and brokenhearted as our reconnection made us feel, we both agree. A documentary needs to be made. We want to help other families like ours and shine the light on solutions where it's been so shadowy and dark for way too long.

Over the next six months, Tommy works really hard to reach goals we didn't know would be attainable in such a short amount of time. Halfway through Tommy's hospitalization, he comes out of his delusion that he is being filmed by satellites. After eighteen months of living in a paranoid nightmare, this is a miraculous moment in all of our lives and in Tommy's recovery.

Telephoning Marilyn and Tyler, we try to explain what's happened and ask them to join us at the hospital. Sitting outside at one of the empty picnic tables, Tommy and Tyler are locked into a conversation, talking to each other nonstop.

We all acknowledge, "It's as if a day hasn't gone by since our families were all together."

Finishing off a couple large pizzas and beverages, Tommy and his Aunt Marilyn speak of how inspirational it feels to be working together again. After dinner, Marilyn gets permission to film inside the hospital so that she can document Tommy's progress, wanting to share this achievement and his optimal buoyancy and resilience with the world. With the camera rolling, Marilyn is shooting a close up of Tommy and instructs him to look at the green light. Tommy begins to explain how real a delusion feels, "especially when a person is in one." Basking in the miracle of this moment, our boy seems to have returned to us from the fringes of insanity and our prodigal son has found his way home once more.

As Tommy continues to thrive with regular treatment at Sylmar, we look into a transitional housing program that Tommy's social worker recommends, called Casa Esperanza. The facility is situated just down the road from the Channel Islands University, which used to be Camarillo State Hospital, the largest state mental hospital in the world upon its completion in 1936.

A few words about the history of our current mental health systems...

Even though the Camarillo State Hospital officially closed in 1997, it was actually President Kennedy that initiated the closure of big mental health lockdown facilities because he felt they lacked compassion. President Kennedy felt that in-home care, versus larger mental hospitals, would be less expensive and kinder to its clients. Sadly, he never fulfilled his vision of creating compassionate care for the mentally ill before his assassination.

President Carter also tried to deinstitutionalize the mentally ill by creating a categorical shift away from diagnosis and treatment facilities, and instead focusing on the role of environment, community social services, and prevention. Federal funds for mental health services were redirected from state hospitals to Community Mental Health Centers (CMHCs). As a result, hundreds of thousands of patients with chronic mental illness were released from state lockdown hospitals to local CMHCs, nursing homes, and board-and-care facilities. The goal was to restore dignity to mental health patients in response to the neglect and mismanagement of state hospital care. However, CMHCs failed to improve the standard of patient care. Under the Mental Health Systems Act, patients had more autonomy to choose whether they take their medications and which services they want to receive. But this is an unrealistic responsibility for people who clearly cannot make sound decisions for themselves. With this increased freedom and integration into society, crime spiked in local communities, and jails and prisons were flooded with the mentally ill.

Prior to this, while serving as the Governor of California, Ronald Reagan had already virtually abolished involuntary hospitalization in California, except in the most extreme cases. By the early 1970s, California had already moved most mentally ill patients out of its state hospitals. When Ronald Reagan became president in 1981, he instituted a disastrous shut down of state mental hospitals without mandatory patient follow ups. The result? Patients were not receiving the care they needed, creating a new influx of unemployment, homelessness, and crime.

So it is this legal, medical and social landscape that we find ourselves in as we consider options for our son.

Tommy's social worker set up a scheduled tour for us at the Casa Esperanza facility.

The director, a pleasant man in his mid-fifties says, "Please come into my office and sit down. Here at Casa we take mental health and recovery very seriously. It's our life's work and passion. Trained therapists work with our clients, and we have trained staff that are available around the clock to dispense meds or help someone if there's a problem. We are here to assist all levels of needs. For our high functioning clients like your son Tommy, if he needs to schedule a medical appointment and he's comfortable doing that, he is welcome to use our office telephone. We are also here to call for him if that makes him feel more comfortable. Once appointments are made, we take our clients to their appointments in our van. Occasionally we make day trips to the beach or the movies, and the clients really seem to enjoy that. Shall we begin the tour?"

We walk to a small house and the director explains, "Our Casa's are coed, and Tommy will be living in this one."

Taking us inside, we are standing in a generous size living room with two couches and coffee tables placed in front of them. There are small, healthy indoor plants in color coordinated ceramic pots that sit on each end table, creating the feeling of a homey, cared-for environment. A big lazy boy recliner takes up one whole corner of the room.

Walking us through an immaculate kitchen the director says, "The clients in this household are responsible for cooking and cleaning in groups. This smaller adjacent room has a television, and we encourage people to watch something positive and agreeable with everyone."

Escorting us to the room that Tommy will occupy, we see a single bed, a closet, a chest of drawers, and a desk. Opening the windows, the director comments, "Great breezes! This corner location of the building has more windows than any of our other private rooms."

He leads us to a small bathroom and says, "This will be Tommy's. You can see it has its own private sink and toilet. We will give him his own room key should he ever want to lock things up." Tom and I exchange glances, silently acknowledging how valuable it would be for Tommy to have such privacy.

Walking out of the Casa and onto the grounds, we enter a generous structure that is enveloped in sunlight. "This is our community room. We play music in here and have dances. Ping pong tournaments, chess boards, and card games are also set up for a fun and relaxing time of socialization. We encourage all our clients to participate in the events.

"Well, that's it, folks!" the director says. "Tommy's room will be available on the day he gets discharged from Sylmar! He is one fortunate fellow to get into our year-long program. Please don't hesitate to call me if you think of any further questions."

Walking back to the car, we are elated with where our son will finish out his treatment. But finding out that the Casa is only a one-year program, we try not to get ahead of ourselves with future housing concerns.

Looking forward to getting out of Sylmar Hospital since the day he entered it, it's the last morning of Tommy's six-month commitment. Against the doctor's wishes, and the director's, Tommy has already packed up his personal belongings and is waiting for our arrival.

"Hello! We are here to pick up our son, Tommy Lennon." The director greets us and asks if he can speak with us privately.

"I need to express my great concern to you both. I feel it would be in Tommy's best interest to stay at Sylmar another six months. He needs that time to stabilize."

Tom explains the dilemma Tommy put us in when he first entered Sylmar–that if we didn't concede to his request of a maximum stay of six months, he promised he would not participate in the program whatsoever and would dispute his conservatorship as soon as possible. The director acknowledges our feelings of being stuck in a dilemma, but reiterates, "This move is not in Tommy's best interest...not right now!"

Tommy is waiting outside the door with his belongings in hand. We tell him what his doctors are recommending and what the director just told us. After hearing us out, he's so upset with this new information, he adamantly says, "No! I'm done! We made a deal! If I stay another day I promise you, it'll be a waste of everyone's time!"

Having never breached a commitment with any of our children, and knowing Tommy would do exactly what he said, we fearfully and reluctantly agree to his release. Many patients gather around Tommy to say goodbye and thank him for being their friend. Staff members express their gratitude for his help when they needed it. But now we are feeling deep heaviness, remorse, and even grief for the decision that we made before Tommy even entered the Sylmar program.

Settling into his new home at the Casa, Tommy continues to grow in the program. We drive out to Camarillo weekly to visit, pick him up for lunch, run errands, or just hang out.

Whenever we arrive, people in the program wander over to us, perhaps out of curiosity, loneliness or both. Tommy begins to complain that both the residents and the staff have come to expect the kindness and leadership traits that come so naturally to him. With the added pressure of leading groups and helping assist the more debilitated clients on outings, he acknowledges the small seeds of resentments that are beginning to grow. "I'm here for my own recovery and support too!"

When Tommy takes a prescribed medicine called Lithium, his symptoms of mental illness from his psychotic break are quelled. His undiagnosed Traumatic Brain Injury has its limitations, but what's apparent is that Tommy is no longer dealing with mental illness, which is the primary focus at Casa Esperanza's program. Both Tom and I are completely aware that Tommy desperately needs to be evaluated and placed in a cognitive Traumatic Brain Injury rehabilitation program, but is there such a thing accessible to him? Or does such a thing even exist?

Tom does the research and discovers only *one facility* out of state, but it costs many thousands of dollars every month to live there and get treatment. Who can afford this? Desperately trying to find a way to get our son help, we research County resources and insurance company benefits to see if they can get involved with TBI diagnosis, treatment, and rehabilitation. But it doesn't exist. We are stonewalled.

Visit after visit, we clearly witness Tommy becoming independently stronger and more educated in his own recovery. There are certain elements of the program that benefit both the brain-injured and the mentally ill, such as structure, regular meals, medication in the proper dosage, and accountability. His performance level is growing head and shoulders above the other clientele there, but we acknowledge that the Casa does provide much-needed consistency for Tommy.

Chapter 21

A Familiar Telephone Conversation

After several weeks of thriving at the Casa, Tommy becomes restless and doesn't want to return to the program after his home visits. He wants to spend more and more time at the house with family instead of participating in the program. His requests for overnights are getting turned down because the program needs to set a limit on how often he can be away. Otherwise, Tommy's spot could be easily filled by someone else in need.

We become acutely aware of the need to balance the time Tommy spends at the program and the time he wants to spend at home. We began to refuse Tommy's increasing requests to come home, but that doesn't stop him from asking. Tommy feels like the program has stopped taking his need to be with family seriously, and it doesn't take long before Tommy stops taking the program seriously.

Sometimes the staff telephones and asks us for his whereabouts. Everyone becomes concerned when we say, "We have no idea, since we assume he is at the program when he isn't with us." Where's Tommy?

Sometimes he's out past curfew, missing his evening meal and medication. Or he leaves early in the morning, missing his breakfast and morning medicine. Sometimes he is gone for most of the day, and no one knows where he is. Tommy's new behavior isn't sitting well with the director, the staff, or us.

Soon after the Casa updates us on Tommy's inconsistencies in the program, Tommy informs us, "I haven't been at the program regularly because I've been looking for rentals, and I've found one! There's an independent living situation at a hotel in downtown Ventura that rents rooms to people like me, on low-income budgets! It's near Narcotics Anonymous meetings, the Mental Health Clinic, a pharmacy, markets, restaurants, the beach, and it's only ten minutes away from you guys!"

He is certain, or more like adamant, that this new arrangement will benefit him more than the Camarillo program he feels he has outgrown. Now his perseveration has kicked in, and his injured impulse control area of his brain is running the show. So once again, if we don't give Tommy his way, he threatens to contest his conservatorship. Game on.

Tommy knows a judge will rule in his favor and legally set him free to do as he pleases. We are completely unprepared for any of this, and yet here we are at another crossroad. We desperately need his conservatorship to remain in place to deter arrests and to prevent the abuse of his human rights if he's incarcerated. Legally speaking, conservatorship is our guiding light through an otherwise dark and challenging reality for our son.

When the Casa Esperanza program director telephones us, he hesitates a moment before delivering information we have heard one too many times before.

"Tommy's a really great guy. Everyone here seems enamored with him and really cares about him, but he has to want to be here. Perhaps another time. We suggest you pack up Tommy's belongings and move him out of our facility as soon as possible. We have a waiting list of people who do want to be here."

As the wind gets knocked out of our sails once again, we acknowl-edge Casa's need for Tommy to want to participate. The decision to have Tommy leave the program has been made for us. We consider having Tommy come home and live with us, but he doesn't want to do that.

"I just want to be free. I haven't been free in years. Can I please rent a room at the Hamilton Hotel?"

Although he is technically making a request, we know that if we say no or ask to look at an alternative living arrangement, he would still get his way. Normally we would never tolerate this demanding behavior, but since Tommy is well over eighteen, and his conservatorship is created for young people who can contest it every six months, we find ourselves yielding to his demands.

CHAPTER 22

THE SAME THING
OVER AND OVER

Moving Tommy from the Camarillo program into his new living quarters at the Hamilton Hotel in Ventura takes some organizing. The hotel has community showers just like at Casa Esperanza, so his showering supplies are already organized in a small carrying container. We gather some linens and extra kitchen items from our home, a couple bowls, plates, glasses, cups, silverware, a pot, a pan, and we purchase a small, affordable microwave. While I go marketing, Tommy gets busy organizing his clothing, art supplies, and other personal items.

Tom builds and installs a long wooden shelf above the sink area in Tommy's tiny kitchen. He also drills a few small holes with screws to hold large hooks. One he attaches inside the closet for Tommy's robe, a few more he installs behind the entry door which holds his jacket, backpack, and a showering towel. We fill his pantry and mini refrigerator with four- or five-days' worth of healthy foods and beverages. A small bowl of seasonal fruit sits on a wooden table for two.

By evening Tom is putting the finishing touches on Tommy's space. He screws in a small dish towel hook next to the dish rack, hangs a paper towel dispenser above his tiny food prep station, and places a cutting board on the counter. When we are all done with the details of moving in, we step back and take a few moments to admire a long day's work. Tommy's new living situation is organized, welcoming, and functional.

He wants to attend a new Twelve Step meeting nearby, and Tom and I are ready to drive home, eat some dinner, and call it a day. Walking downstairs and out to the street level, his Twelve Step meeting is directly across the street!

"Well Tommy, this is it! Congratulations!"

We hug goodnight and tell Tommy how proud we are of him for all of his hard work at the hospital and the Casa, for having found a nearby rental, and for pursuing his dreams of freedom and making them happen.

"Thanks so much, Mom and Dad, for all you did to make this happen. I love you both so much."

"We love you too, Tommy."

The following day we are feeling emotionally and physically beat from the day before. Not hearing from Tommy feels normal. We assume he's having a low-key day too, just like us. Maybe he'll attend a morning or an evening meeting? Maybe both? Perhaps he's napping? Or enjoying life living two blocks from the beach. He could be down at the ocean surfing right now! But instead, we get a disconcerting telephone call from the hotel's night watch manager.

"Mr. Lennon, I need to speak with you and your wife in person. How soon can you get here?"

The manager buzzes us in and tells us, "Your son, Tommy, is not following our hotel protocol. The proper way to visit the hotel is to ring people inside through our front door. Apparently, your son is allowing his visitors to climb in through the fire escape window which is near his room on the second floor."

When we knock on Tommy's door, he calls out, "Just a minute!"

Opening the door, he looks exhausted and disheveled. His room looks like a bomb detonated in there. Dirty dishes and utensils littered the floor and the sink area. Chips and cereal are crushed into the carpet, some clothing and personal items strewn about.

"Yeah, a lot of my belongings are gone."

Above the sink, his pantry shelf is completely emptied. Wondering if there is any food left in his fridge, I look over at it.

"It's empty," he says, nodding at the refrigerator. "I stopped taking my medication when I was at the program and started smoking a little marijuana. My first night here I never made it to the meeting, but it's not going to happen again. I know I messed up. My plan is to get some sleep, get this place cleaned up, go to a meeting, then call you."

We encourage him, "Well, why don't you go ahead and do that. We'll check back in with you later."

On the ground floor walking back out to our car, we ask each other, "How could he have unraveled so quickly?!"

With remorse we remember the Sylmar doctor and director when they reiterated, *"We don't advise Tommy to leave our program at this time. He needs another six months to stabilize."*

Back home, we get through the rest of our afternoon without incident when well into our dinner hour, we get another call from the hotel manager.

"Your son is out of control. He's still allowing people to enter the hotel through the fire escape. If you don't do something, I have no other choice than to call the police."

We meet Mark Stadler at the hotel and explained the situation with Tommy. Mark goes into Tommy's room to speak with him. A few minutes later, Mark returns to the lobby where we are waiting and tells us that during their conversation, Tommy was very polite, respectful and charming as he can be at times. Mark explains that there wasn't cause to take him based on the behavior he had observed. I then ask him to talk to Tommy about the cameras that are filming his life story. Mark says, "Seriously?"

Mark and his CIT officers return to Tommy's room, and within minutes, they are back downstairs with Tommy handcuffed. Mark says as soon as they started talking about the cameras, Tommy became a different person that needed a mental health examination. The officers take Tommy back to the Hillmont Acute Care Psychiatric Hospital. Because Tommy is still on conservatorship, he is stabilized and transferred back to Sylmar's long term psychiatric lockdown facility.

Tommy is very upset to be back in the Sylmar hospital. When he finally calls us, he says, "I was so angry with you both that you put me back in here, I needed time to cool down." Then he asks us, "Can you please come down here and visit me? Maybe we can have dinner together if you want to stop and get burgers or something?"

Utterly exhausted, we draw a line in the sand. "No. We've had enough! We need time to recover. We've been down at the hotel all day."

"What for?"

"We had the remainder of the month to pack up the last of your belongings, which we did. Today we were patching and painting to get our cleaning deposit refunded."

"When do you think you'll feel like visiting?"

"Right now, we've no idea."

We need to process the chain of events that led him out of Sylmar, then Casa Esperanza, then the Hamilton Hotel, then back to Hillmont hospital and eventually back to Sylmar hospital. The cyclical nature of Tommy's psychotic breaks makes us want to jump on a plane to a faraway place and never return. We seriously begin to question if our efforts are accomplishing anything.

Several weeks later, we drive to the Sylmar Hospital with an early dinner of hamburgers, fries, and chocolate shakes. Tommy comes out from the hospital ward into the waiting room and greets us both with a hug. Tommy was sweet as always, and his demeanor was cooperative but with little conversation, which is unlike him.

After eating his dinner, Tommy steps outside to have a cigarette. He opens the plate glass door, and chilly air engulfs us all. We watch him try to light a ciggy by cupping his hands around it. Drawing in a long pull then exhaling, Tommy cautiously looks around and begins to walk away. The only thing left lingering is a trail of smoke.

Tom quickly gets up from the table to see which direction Tommy is headed. Tommy picks up his stride and begins skipping every other step up to the parking lot level, then he breaks into a jog.

We notify the hospital staff that Tommy Lennon has left the premises. Before we leave the facility, the hospital puts out a missing person's report to the police.

"We'll contact you as soon as we find him or hear anything. Please, do the same!"

On our way home, we both acknowledge the whole "I miss you, come visit me" plea was a ploy to get us out there so he could escape. When we arrive home, we call the hospital, but no word has come in yet. Every time we call the hospital to inquire about our son, they have nothing, no information. Our relentless question persists: Where's Tommy?

Three days go by and still no update. Desperate to know his whereabouts we call hospitals, emergency rooms, jails, and morgues all around that area.

Finally on day five, we get a collect call from Tommy. He is disoriented and doesn't know where he is. Tom instructs him to ask people passing by to tell him what city he is in and what street he is on. He asks Tommy to describe what is around him or if he sees any numbers on buildings. Tom gathers enough information to start looking for Tommy. I stay home by the telephone in case Tommy calls again. Tom continues to stop at random telephone booths and occasionally checks in with me, "Have you heard anything from Tommy yet?"

Many hours go by when Tom finally calls to say, "I found him! In Los Angeles! He's in bad shape. I'm bringing him home, then he's going to need to see a doctor."

Tommy's face and head are so violently beaten, they are misshapen. When we ask him about it, he replies with a painfully inappropriate smile, "My friends did this to me."

I call Sylmar Hospital and tell them, "My husband Tom found our son Tommy. We will bring him back to the hospital after we get him in to see a doctor for his injuries."

At the emergency room, a doctor examines Tommy's eyes for proof of concussion and checks his face and skull, but sees no reason to order an x-ray. He releases Tommy with a pat on the back, and an anecdotal prescription, "Stay out of trouble!"

Finally back home with Tommy resting, we get a call from the director at Sylmar. "We will not be readmitting your son to our hospital unless you surrender Tommy's conservatorship to the County. That way we will have full authority over his recovery."

Though Tom and I know the value of maintaining conservatorship, we agree to transfer the conservatorship from Tom to the County of Ventura. Our biggest issue with transferring Tommy's conservatorship to the County is that it gives Tommy the opportunity to contest his conservatorship.

Although the directors at Sylmar Hospital and the Ventura County Conservator's Office assure us of a successful outcome, someone mistakenly contacts the wrong doctor to testify at Tommy's hearing.

This doctor is from the Hillmont Acute Psychiatric Care Hospital in Ventura. Tommy's most current psychiatrist from the lockdown facility at Sylmar never shows up at the hearing. The slipshod method of transferring Tommy's conservatorship from Tom Sr. to the County is taking place in the main hallway outside of a Ventura County Courtroom. In this very public hallway, Tom and I stand before a judge and are told that we would not be allowed to speak on behalf of Tommy's compelling case history. The judge informs us that medical and criminal history is not permitted in young people's conservatorship cases, and that it's all about how the person is doing *at that moment.*

Without Tommy's treating doctors from Sylmar, who would have presented the most current information, the judge makes the declaration, "Thomas Patrick Lennon Jr. you are competent, and you're free to go your own way."

The judge releases Tommy without any further ado or follow up care. Upon hearing this news, Tommy leaps from his chair, pumping both fists in the air like a weightlifter. As he walks away, he gloats with every rep, "Yes! Yes! Yes!"

Tom calls out, "Hey! Where are you going?"

Tommy gleefully touts, "To live in the Ventura River bottom. *I am a free man!*"

Tommy's history needed to be heard, along with CIT police records, and the testimony of his latest treating doctors. If that could have occurred, it's obvious that people like our son, Tommy, could remain under the assistance and the umbrella of a lifelong conservatorship. Instead, our son's fate–determined in a public hallway outside the courtroom, with a judge listening to the testimony of the wrong doctor, while forbidding us to speak about Tommy's history–allows our son the freedom of homelessness.

For nearly a year and half while Tommy remained under conservatorship with his dad, he was never arrested nor placed in the criminal justice system. Now we are afraid for Tommy and so angry at the system. No matter how many times we request Tommy's medical records, the prison never sends them. Then soon after we lose the conservatorship, we get a telephone call from two Ventura police officers who know Tommy well.

"Your son has been illegally camping in the river bottom, and he's not doing well mentally. He's talking but not making a lot of sense. Should we take him to the Hillmont Hospital instead of arresting him?"

Knowing he is in desperate need of help, we gratefully agree to have Tommy taken to Hillmont, thinking this is a godsend, an intervention, a pivotal moment. We believe maybe we can conserve our son again.

But after speaking with the County Conservator's Office, we are now informed that the County conserving Tommy is now financially out of the question.

"It takes so many county workers to oversee cases and clients, plus we no longer have the staff or funding to conserve people. If your son isn't in extremely critical condition, meaning borderline insane, or a threat to himself, society or both, conservatorship is no longer an option."

"Even if we are his conservators?"

The conservator's office concludes our request with their grim forecast, "If your son can feed himself out of a trash can or take shelter under a bridge, he's competent enough to take care of himself."

The whole situation seems incomprehensible. After all the professional involvement and money spent on Tommy's recovery, we stand helpless as we watch his conservatorship, medical solutions, and medication all evaporate into ether.

CHAPTER 23

FORCED INTO
OTHER REALMS

One evening while listening to a radio program, Tom hears about a book by award-winning journalist Jim Robbins called *Symphony in the Brain: The Evolution of the New Brain Wave Biofeedback*. He buys and reads the book with the possibility of using neurofeedback treatment for our son. Tom suspects he's on the trail of something significant, a profound shift in the way Tommy's recovery could be understood and approached.

After researching practitioners in our area, Tom discovers Ventura social worker, Cynthia Smith. Tom and Cynthia connect over their mutual passion for neurofeedback and work out a trade arrangement. Tom will go to her office to practice with her equipment and learn how to set up training protocols under her watchful eye. Once familiar with her protocols, Tom can treat her clients while she takes a sabbatical in Europe. In exchange, Tom can use her office and equipment to train our son, Tommy.

Tom keeps a journal of his training sessions with Cynthia, and also notes his progress with Tommy:

> *I learn where to attach electrodes to the scalp at specific locations. The brain emits microvolts of energy, and these are picked up by the electrodes and fed into an amplifier that sends them to a computer program, which filters out*

the various frequencies and displays them on the comput-
er screen. I then set up a protocol to accomplish our goals for
that session. Generally, we inhibit slow frequencies (they
make it difficult to focus), reward medium frequencies
(better focus, calming), and inhibit fast frequencies (hy-
persensitivity, edginess). This is done by setting thresholds
for each frequency, then a bell sounds when that criterion
is met. In other words, when the brain meets all three
frequency criteria at the same time, a reward bell chimes.
It's called 'operant conditioning' (like Pavlov's dog).

Different areas (lobes) of the brain are locations for a
variety of symptoms that we address. I first used it to
help Tommy control the involuntary shaking of his hands
and legs caused by the medications they gave him in the
psychiatric hospitals. It works quite well and makes him
a "believer." He also tells me that he's begun dreaming
again after several months of not dreaming. We've got
a regimen of three sessions per week, with each session
lasting twenty minutes. Tommy really likes how it makes
him feel. Consistently, we see the behavioral calming
effects.

Around the same time, Tom reads an article by Dr. Walker, MD, who's the president of the Association for Applied Psychophysiology and Biofeedback. Tom sends him this letter:

Dear Dr. Walker,

While reading your "Letter from the President" in Neuro Connections, *I am particularly struck by the state-
ment that you make, your belief that "...we could almost
empty our prisons with neurofeedback, and truly reha-
bilitate those in our prison system."*

Tom then joins the much-respected Peter Van Deusen's email list of
practitioners for brain training, which includes MDs, PhDs, nurses,
clinicians, and other students of neurofeedback. After Tom consults
with Clinical Director Sue Othmer at the EEG (electroencephalogra-
phy) Spectrum Clinic, he again writes to Dr. Walker about his work
with Tommy:

*Sue is consulting with me as to the appropriate protocols
to address the most salient issues of my son's dilemma,
alleviating the many side effects from taking medication.*

Tommy reports that the neurofeedback treatments put him in a
restful state. With such a positive result, Tom continues his education
and takes one of Van Deusen's clinical training class. Tom also vol-
unteers at a weekend neurofeedback seminar, helping with set-up and
running a film projector in exchange for attending their classes. He
meets with several of the top practitioners. When he calls me from his
hotel room later that evening, I can hear the smile in his voice.

"They even offered to give me specific protocols that should help
Tommy!"

Hearing the excitement in Tom's voice, I am reminded of a quote by Gautama Buddha, "Your purpose in life is to find your purpose, and give your whole heart and soul to it."

After discussing neurofeedback with a new acquaintance named Helga, they decide to make a trade–neurofeedback sessions in exchange for an astrological reading. Although we may have reservations about the *science* of astrology, we both do feel that some people have the Gift of Sight. Helga has a bachelor's degree in physics, a master's in mythology, and a reputation in both our small town and around the globe for excellence and accuracy in her readings.

As we meet with Helga over tea, she sees something of concern in my chart. "Debbie, do you have a child falling into unfamiliar territory with medicine, doctors or institutions?"

"Oh my gosh!!! Yes! Our family is being forced out of Western Medicine."

"Why?"

I explain about the surfing accident, the forensic psychiatrist at Twin Towers telling us about Traumatic Brain Injury, and how Tommy is incapable of functioning properly.

"We, ourselves, made the grave mistake of removing our son from a psychiatric lockdown facility too early. Tommy's conservatorship is no longer in place. The County of Ventura vacated it. At every turn, as we try to get him appropriate help, we feel like we're hitting a rock wall."

"I understand, perhaps more than you can possibly imagine. While my brother was temporarily living in a mental institution where he had placed himself, his doctor instructed the staff to administer heavy doses of an antipsychotic medication on a daily basis. This dosage eventually resulted in an unnecessary, fatal reaction. Maybe, just maybe,

Tommy and your family have been spared from the very tragic loss that our family lives with every day."

After a pause, Helga then shared, "My father was a dentist who frequently volunteered his services to the Tule River Indian tribe, located in the flat plains outside of Fresno. Maybe their Medicine Man might work with your son, even though Tommy is under forty years of age and, therefore, too young to become a Shaman."

"A Shaman?"

Helga explains, "Shamanism is a perspective and an honor. Shamans have a gift of foreseeing a luminous future or foreshadowing. Different cultures regard the Shaman as a priest or priestess known to use magic for the purpose of divining the hidden and curing the sick. A person cannot become a Shaman until the age of forty because their life callings and experiences on this earth usually take them out first. If they live to be forty years old, then the Shaman's job is to go out to the peripherals of the land, reporting back to the tribe the visions they've experienced while sojourning in and out of different perspectives."

Maybe Helga is onto something. Now that Tommy is an adult and is resistant to taking prescribed medication because of its debilitating side effects—shaking, slurred speech, blurry vision and weight gain—perhaps this is an opportunity to incorporate alternative views and embrace the gift of a culture we know little about, the Native American Indians.

Helga makes it clear that communicating by telephone to the reservation is no easy task. But eventually a healing ceremony for Tommy gets scheduled. Even though Tommy is under forty years of age, the Medicine Man with the incongruous name of Clarence does this favor for Helga because her father is so revered.

When Tom asks Helga, "How do I pay Clarence?"

She answers, "Bring tobacco. If it feels appropriate, a cash donation. Whatever you feel is right for you."

After Tommy and Tom return from their all-day journey to the Medicine Man, I greet them with curiosity and eagerly ask, "How did it go? Tell me all about it!"

Tom explains, "We found the reservation without difficulty. Driving onto the Tule tribe's land, we saw a couple of dogs, known as greeters. We later found out they are called painted dogs, painted wolves or singing dogs. Apparently they are *the* most efficient hunters. Anyway, they led us to Clarence. He was waiting for us outside his cobb dwelling. He is a man of few words and a very gentle presence. Lighting a very large bundle of sage, he encircled us with smoke, clearing any unwanted energy. Carrying the sage over to the entrance of his cobb dwelling, he motioned for us to step over the wooden threshold into his...I don't know what you'd call it, a medicine hut? Shelves were covered with peculiar shaped stones, wooden objects, feathers, claws, hair figurines, and representations of the sun. There's all these medicinal plants, some I had never heard of before like cinchona for blood disorders and Jalapa, which he told us is for when a child is good all day but cries at night."

Seated together at our circular table, Tom pauses to take a sip from his steaming cup of tea before continuing.

"Clarence then started his work on Tommy. When the ceremony began, it was so loud at times that my ears felt assaulted! But it was like a good pain, like getting a splinter removed or something. Clarence directed this loud disturbance towards all the evil spirits thought to cause sickness. He called in the good spirits to alleviate and cure conditions or symptoms. Songs were sung invoking the aid of the Great Spirit. Clarence's eyes were closed while chanting prayers and shaking different rattles. His feet moved like a bear stomping to give a warning before charging. Oh, it was really an intense experience! But the momentum that was building felt...purifying. When Clarence reached this crescendo of sounds and movement, at the highest point in the ceremony, he placed his hand on Tommy's forehead–I mean right on his injury! It's like he sensed exactly where the surfboard struck him, not even knowing the location."

Tommy, excitedly wanting to tell the rest of the story, jumps in, "Yeah! With this crazy, huge voice, Clarence made a command that all the great spirits help me. Then he called out my name, 'TOMMY!' Then he just kept saying over and over, 'Tommy come back! Tommy! Tommy! Return!'

"Like instantly I felt Clarence's power work! My anxiety disappeared, and I felt like I was just letting go of bad things. My heart felt so peaceful. Mom, I just couldn't thank him enough!"

Long term, we don't know exactly what the ceremony will accomplish regarding Tommy's Traumatic Brain Injury, but at this point in our journey, we like to think every alternative approach can possibly serve a cumulative purpose. And there are worse things than a short-lived peace.

CHAPTER 24

PRECIOUS FAMILY MOMENTS

While Tommy is in a fairly stable state, Kim and I plan the final details of their son Elijah's visit to California. We can't wait for him to join us on our family reunion camp-out!

Arriving at the Los Angeles Airport, Tom, Tommy, and I can hardly contain our cheerfulness! As we see our handsome 12-year-old young man with his duffle bag in hand, we all call out at the same time, "There he is!!"

We all embrace, forming a circle of long-awaited hugs. Tommy and Elijah have mirror grins on their sweet faces, and my heart feels like it could explode! After a quick stop at the drive through for burgers and fries, we are homeward bound, excited to leave early the next morning for our sun-drenched camping destination, Lake Nacimiento.

When we arrive midday at the lake, Tommy's siblings and all of their kids gather around Elijah, taking turns giving him bear hugs with laughter. Our larger Lennon family of aunts, uncles, and cousins are already out on the lake water skiing, swimming, and fishing, while back at the camp, others are making meals altogether.

Every evening before sunset, we form a huge circle of camp chairs around the campfire. There must be fifty of us snuggled together around that fire! We roast marshmallows and make gooey smores while Tom and his brother tune their guitars. Soon they are accompanying beautiful family harmonies to songs from the 1960s, like Simon and Garfunkel's "Scarborough Fair" and Louis Armstrong's "What a Wonderful World." It reminds me of my first camp trip with the Lennon's when I met Tom for the first time. It's just magic.

After spending our last morning out on the lake swimming and skiing, we break down our camp and bid farewell to our dear loved ones. Filled to the brim with love and connection with our larger family, we're eager to have some quiet time back home since there's only a couple of days left of Elijah's visit.

Once we are home, Tommy is no longer behaving as consistently as he was at the lake. Picking up some marijuana, his behavior begins to fracture. Marijuana, which may seem innocuous to most people these days, affects Tommy in an over-the-top, manic way. He becomes harder to deal with. He'll purposely give no response to a question I've asked, or 'yes' me, so that I'll just be quiet. Tom and I begin to wonder if his lack of impulse control will make him want to continue using marijuana for the rest of Elijah's visit. But the loving bond between father and son appears to be so substantial, outstanding, and meaningful, somehow Tommy is able to refrain, and we are all spared.

On Elijah's last day, the two-hour ride to the Los Angeles airport is spent with him and Tommy chatting in the backseat until we reach our destination. They even make plans for Elijah to visit three months from now during his winter break.

After heartening goodbyes, we watch Elijah walk down the hallway to his boarding gate. Elijah turns around for one last endearing glimpse, and our eyes fill to the brim with tears. Walking out of the airport and back to our car, Tommy comments about how he's already missed out on so much of Elijah's life. It makes me wonder if maybe some part of Tommy knows that he can't guarantee anything for their future either.

On the last leg of our journey back home, Tommy asks if we would please stop the car and drop him off in Ventura. With so few hours left of daylight, we question his request, but Tommy insists we drop him off.

"Thanks for understanding, I just need to be at the beach. I need some time to myself to reflect on my time with Elijah."

CHAPTER 25
CATCH 22

Tommy doesn't return home that evening but calls the next day and says, "I hitchhiked north to Santa Barbara! It only took me like forty-five minutes to get here! I don't know how long I'll stay. But please don't worry about me, I've got a lot of friends that I can stay with."

"Who are they?"

"Oh, they're from the Homeless Nation." That's how he likes to refer to all his homeless friends.

A couple weeks later we get a call from Tracey, a psychiatric court liaison at the Santa Barbara Acute Psychiatric Hospital.

"Your son, Thomas, has been arrested and found incompetent to stand trial."

"Why was he arrested?"

"Apparently, he found a wig in a dumpster, put it on his head, and wore it into a women's public bathroom, thinking that it was funny. Someone reported him. He also tested positive for methamphetamine."

Her words twist my stomach into knots. This is the first time I have ever heard of methamphetamine. My only reference to it is from news stories of makeshift meth labs that blow up in people's houses, and images of haggard addicts with missing teeth. How will this new drug affect Tommy's life with a brain injury?

We want to help Tracey better understand Tommy's brain-injured behavior, so Tom tells her the story of one of the most famous neuroscience patients ever, a railroad foreman named Phineas Gage (1823-1860).

"While preparing a railroad bed, using an iron tamping rod to pack an explosive powder into a hole, it detonated, and the rod went through Phineas' cheek and skull. It was a seemingly unsurvivable accident. He survived, but with damage to the frontal lobe of his brain. This affected his judgment, impulse control, sexual behavior, and overall social abilities. He was transformed into a surly, aggressive, heavy drinker, unable to hold down a job.

"Even today, scientists don't really know how the prefrontal lobes exercise control. Someone with a prefrontal injury can still pass most neurological exams with flying colors. Pretty much anything you can measure in the lab—memory, language, motor skills, reasoning, intelligence—can seem intact. It's only outside the lab that problems can be seen. In particular, personalities change. And people with prefrontal damage often show a lack of ambition, foresight, empathy, and other hard-to-measure traits. These aren't the kind of things a stranger would notice right away. But family and friends are acutely aware that something is off. Tracey, this is what our son, Tommy, is dealing with. He's not a criminal."

With information we provide to the Santa Barbara Acute Psychiatric Hospital about Tommy's surfing accident and subsequent behavioral changes, they then assess that Tommy has an undiagnosed TBI.

This turns out to be a double-edged sword.

"Tommy's conservatorship was just recently vacated," Tom informs Tracey. "Can he be conserved and stay in treatment, since he is already there?"

"No," she replies. "Tommy can't get a conservatorship in Santa Barbara, because his primary diagnosis is Traumatic Brain Injury. There is nothing set up for TBI in our mental health system."

Catch 22. We are again at a loss for direction.

While Tommy waits in the Santa Barbara Psych Ward to be transferred to Patton State Hospital (a lockdown hospital for criminals), he calls us one day and says, "I was watching television in here, and I saw myself dancing on TV!"

At first, this sounds frighteningly similar to one of his delusions, but it really did happen!

Aunt Marilyn Braverman's film about Tommy, *A Revolving Door*, had gained national attention in the film world and was nominated to short-list for an Academy Award in 2007 for Best Short Documentary. It also aired on HBO's "Addiction" series for a month, and that's when Oprah's people called our home.

On three separate occasions, Oprah's staff call and ask Tom, Tommy, and I to appear on a schizophrenic show, a bipolar show, and then to share an hour-long show on drug addiction with the author of a book called *Beautiful Boy: A Father's Journey Through His Son's Addictions*. However, we decline their invitations, each time asking, "Is it possible to do a Traumatic Brain Injury show?"

We express how extremely dedicated we are to shedding light on this severe problem in our social system.

"It's Traumatic Brain Injuries that are keeping our prisons and jails full to capacity. TBIs have been around as long as humans have been around, and we still have such limited resources to help deal with them. Can you help us?"

But Oprah's people inform us, "We have assignments to fulfill. We are sorry we cannot accommodate you. People just aren't ready for a brain injury show right now. It's not a popular topic, and when we do have a call for it, we will be sure and call you."

We still haven't heard back from Oprah's company about a TBI episode, but they nonetheless use some of Tommy's film footage from his documentary to advertise one of their own programs on addiction! Tommy's life ended up on TV afterall, and that is what Tommy saw in the patient lounge at the hospital that day.

Meanwhile, before Tommy is sent to Patton State Hospital, the Santa Barbara Court liaison, Tracey, writes a letter to the Santa Barbara Superior Court to clearly describe Tommy's dilemma.

> *Mr. Lennon has a significant brain injury which has caused frontal lobe brain damage. This part of the brain is responsible for executive functioning, and damage to it would account for his lack of judgment, poor impulse control, inability to plan things out in a step-by-step fashion, or follow through with things, despite his intentions to do so. Unfortunately, his prognosis is poor. It is unlikely, due to his underlying brain damage, that medication can help. He off and on maintains a belief that his life is being recorded in order to help others who are being hospitalized and incarcerated against their will.*

Apparently letters like this one have no bearing on developing a treatment plan for Tommy that focuses on TBI, and instead he is finally transferred to Patton State Hospital to be treated for mental illness, but what about treatment for his TBI?

Once transferred, Tommy is never court ordered to take medication. We call the court liaison in Santa Barbara to ask, "How is Tommy supposed to become competent enough to appear before a judge if he isn't put on some kind of medication for his delusions?"

She tells us, "I don't know. He was on medication when we sent him to Patton."

"So, what's going to happen to him?" Once again, we are left with more questions than answers.

CHAPTER 26
PATTON STATE HOSPITAL

Tom Sr. arranges for us to have a private meeting with the director of Patton State Hospital to discuss the possibility of using neurofeedback there to treat our son. In exchange, Tom offers to donate his time and services to help treat other inmates who could possibly benefit from the various neurofeedback protocols.

"Unfortunately, I cannot allow that in our facility," the director replies, "but we did try it here once."

Tom, clearly impressed that they had tried it, asks, "What kind of results did you get?"

"Well I personally witnessed one incorrigible prisoner, who had to be restrained all hours of the day, and this guy clearly benefited from neurofeedback treatments. This was many years ago, but I've just recently heard that he still has not been returned to the criminal system and is doing well."

Even with the obvious success the director had witnessed, he says that neurofeedback is still not an approved part of their treatment plan. Deeply disappointed to be turned down, Tom and I could only speculate that the drug companies would not want prisoners using such a natural, inexpensive, and powerful tool like neurofeedback, because there would no longer be a need for a massive distribution of pharmaceuticals. Banning neurofeedback after such a successful story at Patton just doesn't make sense to us.

A few weeks after our meeting about neurofeedback, we get a call from the director of the hospital.

"Your son has been arrested out of our facility and is in Rancho Cucamonga Jail. He's there on a felony for a gassing charge."

We have no idea what gassing means, and ask.

"Your son went into a manic cycle and started singing and dancing nonstop. The staff felt they had but only one choice, and that was to restrain Tommy and administer a sedative. Your son reacted to the staff person who was restraining him. He spit at the attendant. Exchanging bodily fluids without permission is called *gassing* and it is a felony, punishable by law."

Extremely shocked and surprised by this information, I ask the director, "How is it possible that someone incompetent to stand trial could be arrested for their behavior inside of a mental hospital?"

The director goes on to say, "We have rules here that a prisoner reads and agrees to, and then signs their name. Your son knows the rules, he read them, he signed his name. I will mail you a copy."

Tom and I call our dear friend, Sue Rueb, the founder of the non-profit called B.R.A.I.N. (Brain Rehabilitation and Injury Network). Sue and I met through Dr. Todd Clements, a longtime associate of Dr. Amen, who utilizes the S.P.E.C.T. (Single Photon Emission Computed Tomography) scan. This cutting-edge technology uses a radioactive compound to detect brain injury with high accuracy by showing active brain cells, which emit the most energy, versus injured ones that emit less energy.

As soon as we update Sue and tell her about Tommy getting arrested out of Patton, she immediately contacts her friend, a civil rights lawyer who is also on the board at B.R.A.I.N. and tells him about Tommy's predicament. Within a week of speaking with this dear man, Tommy is released from jail and returned to Patton State Hospital. All charges were dropped.

After spending a few months at Patton State Hospital, Tommy is reported to be stable enough to go before a judge that will sentence him for the Santa Barbara wig episode, but Tom and I begin questioning Tommy's competency. Being affiliated with the Ventura chapter of the National Alliance for Mental Illness for some time, and having actually become one of their spokespersons, I decide to call the local president, William. He also has a son who was sent to Patton Hospital as incompetent to stand trial.

After explaining that Tommy was never put on medication for his delusional thoughts, I question, "How does the treating psychiatrist determine Tommy is suddenly competent to stand trial without medication?"

William informs me, "Patton prompts the incompetent to learn the correct responses to say before a judge, so they can be considered competent to stand trial. In other words, Tommy is being groomed to face a prosecuting attorney who wants to punish Tommy to the full extent of the law."

Knowing this shocking truth sadly doesn't help Tommy's situation. We attend a meeting with Tommy and his public defender minutes before Tommy is to appear before a judge. The public defender tells him, "We can definitely beat this wig charge, but don't think for a minute that what you did is ok!"

Tommy says, "I'm really embarrassed. I didn't mean to harm anyone. I just thought putting on that wig was going to be funny."

"Tommy, your brain injury spells out back-to-back jail and prison sentences over and over again. I hope you can see this now!"

His public defender is losing his patience and speaks so loudly, it seems like there is no attorney-client confidentiality whatsoever.

"You just want to plead guilty so that you can get out of jail without the stress and pressures of a trial? Don't you know that if you don't go to trial to prove your intent was inappropriate humor, it will affect everything else you do for as long as you live?!"

Tommy, only knowing how to live his life in the moment, makes his plea in court before the judge, "I am guilty, Your Honor."

What if he had said, "I am brain injured, Your Honor, and the decision-making area of my brain has been damaged. I have impulse control issues." Do you think maybe then Tommy would have been heard, and the judge might have ordered further testing? Perhaps further testing could prove Tommy had zero malicious intent?

Every year, on every birthday, Tommy will now have to register as a sex offender. If he fails to register on time, he can be imprisoned. But administrative mistakes do happen, and we discover this truth the first time Tommy has to register. Even though his father did take him to register on time, an error in processing falsely recorded Tommy as late. The mistake is later acknowledged by the criminal system in a letter after Tommy innocently served months in a prison cell for a crime he didn't commit.

With Tommy now in his late thirties, he is growing into his manhood with a lust for fun and slightly naughty foolishness. His immature behaviors are interpreted as deliberate, as though he is trying to cause harm to someone. This causes momentous and gravely consequential, life-changing events to happen–like having to register as a sex offender for the rest of his life.

Tragically we are losing Tommy due to the lack of treatment he needs for a TBI. Continuing to plead guilty to charges he isn't truly guilty of, he doesn't realize that the leash of the law just keeps getting shorter and shorter around his neck, like a noose. When Tommy is finally released from incarceration, parole gives their approval for him to live at The Camp, but not without strapping a tracking monitor on his ankle first. Now Tommy is a marked man, singled out as an object of suspicion, judgment and a target for more arrests.

The Camp is an old 1950s motel with several bunk beds to a room and outdoor bathrooms and showers. There's a mess hall with long formica tables where residents are provided three meals a day. We are grateful for this last resort for the downtrodden. It's one of the only places Tommy can live with his limited restrictions, being on parole, and now having to register as a sex offender.

Settling into the residence, Tommy tries a new skateboarding maneuver and sprains his back. Relaxing on his bunk, he thinks he's charging his tracking device, but he doesn't know it's been damaged by his fancy footwork on his skateboard, and it's not taking a charge.

We get a call from his parole agent. "Tommy's tracking monitor has lost a hundred percent of its charge. I have to find him and arrest him for this parole violation. There's no getting around it, it's an automatic 180-day sentence, and IF he behaves while incarcerated, it will get reduced to 90 days."

Hanging up the telephone, I begin to wonder, is there a GPS inside each tracking device? Is that how his agent knows when, and where, and how to find Tommy? Because when parole is looking for Tommy, they find him.

Once when he was using a gas station bathroom out by our local shopping mall, Tommy's battery in his tracker died and parole was waiting for him outside the bathroom ready to arrest him. When Tommy opened the door, they pushed him back inside the men's room, handcuffed him, placed him under arrest and took him to jail.

Is keeping his ankle monitor charged for thirty minutes, twice-a-day an unreasonable task for someone like Tommy? It has the appearance of trying to undermine our son and others like him. I begin to wonder if failing to charge trackers is what's keeping our jails and prisons full to capacity with the brain injured, the mentally ill and the homeless. Tommy is once again behind bars.

One day, our son Jeff tells us about a telephone call he recently received from his dad's older brother, his Uncle Ted.

"I've been thinking about your brother, Tommy. I'm curious, what are your thoughts if I help support Tommy with his art, speaking engagements, or future film projects? I'm thinking if I invest in him, it'll keep him busy, financially productive, and maybe out of jail. How do you feel about asking your brother to write me a wish list of the most important things he would like help with, and we'll see what pans out?"

On our next visit to see Tommy, Jeff tells his brother about his phone call with their Uncle Ted.

Tommy asks, "What does he mean, a wish list?"

Jeff replies, "Exactly that! List the most important things to you, anything you want."

About a week after that visit, Tom and I get an oversized postcard in the mail. It's from the jail. It's Tommy's wish list! On the front of it, Tommy draws a picture of a big cartoonish black and white cat behind bars. A little mouse, who is on the other side of the bars, is holding the key to Tommy's cell door behind its back. Tommy writes:

I wish for my own place with a washing machine, dryer, and a bath.

I wish for food to eat, and someone to cook me hot meals.

I wish I could get a lawyer to help me straighten out my legal matters, and straighten out my S.S.I.

I wish I could get a therapist and a family therapist to help me gain my sanity and reunite with my family.

I also wish I could get a membership to L.A. Fitness to stay focused on my physical well-being as well as my mental well-being.

I wish to be able to visit my son Elijah and his mom Kim in hopes of reuniting as a family.

If I could receive this kind of help financially, I would be eternally grateful.

Sincerely,
Thomas Patrick Lennon Jr.

As requested, Tom forwards the wish list to his older brother Ted. We also share Tommy's list with the rest of the family in hopes that they too will enjoy his humorous artwork and the simplicity and beauty of his wishes.

At every visit Tommy inquires about his wish list and asks if there's going to be a place for him to live when he gets out. Despite everyone's good intentions, there are problems with fulfilling his wish list. Having lived his entire adult life in institutions or amongst the homeless, living in his own space seems to be the most important piece of the puzzle for Tommy's own peace of mind. Knowing that he has his own room with a roof over his head and a door he can close or lock if he wishes to, could bring a sense of balance and dignity back into his life.

But Tommy's reality is even if we were to co-sign a rental lease and financially take on the monthly responsibilities (with his Uncle Ted's generous help), Tommy still won't meet the qualifications needed for a homeowner to want to rent to someone like him. He's been told by law enforcement that it's mandatory to reveal to any potential landlord that he is on parole and that he has to register as a sex offender. Just one of many long-term consequences of Tommy's frontal lobe brain injury. We also cannot forget how many times in his manic episodes, he has trashed his lodgings or just run away.

It seems like our puzzle of how to help our boy is always missing a piece. Nowhere in the criminal system is Tommy *ever* treated as a brain-injured person.

CHAPTER 27

A WELL-DESERVED RANT

Traumatic Brain Injury has long been considered an event that a person survives, which suggests that the person can move beyond or cure their condition. This can happen, but research has shown that TBI is usually not a singular event, but rather the beginning of a chronic, lifelong disability. TBI shortens life expectancy and multiplies the occurrence of seizures, psychiatric disorders, and sleep disorders, to name a few.

Today, too many service members return from our wars with either diagnosed or often undiagnosed TBIs, and they don't understand why they are unable to cope with everyday life. Many men and women no longer recognize themselves or their behaviors. Some lose their marriages, their families, their jobs and close relationships, leaving them to fend for themselves. As we have seen with our Tommy, this can lead to drug abuse and homelessness.

With a proper diagnosis, immediate recommendations for cognitive and behavioral therapies could interrupt the deterioration process for months, or even years, after the initiating traumatic event. If the chronic nature of Traumatic Brain Injury was more fully recognized by governing agencies, they could help direct funding towards more accurate diagnosis. Updating emergency room equipment for head injuries would be a significant start for diagnosing TBIs when they happen.

It's not just the survivors themselves that suffer, it is our society as a whole. Traumatic Brain Injuries are bogging down our mental health and criminal justice systems. A *Newsweek* article from 2016 reveals hard-to-believe statistics about brain injuries in our prison systems. In one randomly picked Colorado criminal facility, over 90 percent of the prisoners surveyed have TBIs. A 2008 study of 990 Minnesota inmates found a rate of 80 percent; a 2006 analysis of 200 Australian prisoners found 82 percent; and a 2007 survey of 107 male and 118 female inmates from six federal prisons found 87 percent. Staggering.

What if our court system would include Traumatic Brain Injury as its own category for the purpose of sentencing? If TBI screening and testing were mandatory before sentencing, judges and public defenders would then be able to weigh the difference between criminals with intent versus those that are suffering from a physical/mental impairment. Separating these two populations would be a great first step forward.

Let's take a quick look at our prison system now...

Private prisons are a multi-billion dollar industry in the United States. Not only does our country have the largest number of prisoners, but we are also home to the highest incarceration rate worldwide. Roughly 2.12 million people were incarcerated in the U.S. in 2020.

The dark truth...if we build jails and prisons for profit, then there will be a need to continually keep them filled with inmates. After all, doesn't a profitable business depend on repeat customers?

This reminds me of our family friend Brett Dennen and his song "Ain't No Reason."

Ain't no reason things are this way,
It's how they've always been and they intend to stay,

*Prison walls still standing tall, some things never change
at all,*
Love will come set me free, love will come set me free.

If only it were that easy.

We sadly have learned too much about the shortcomings of our for-profit prison system.

One problem we've found is that vendors who have contracts with these institutions often charge inmates' families and friends exorbitant prices on a regular basis. When Tom and I put money in Tommy's commissary account, he is able to purchase overpriced calling cards from that facility's telephone carrier, toiletries and extra food. We worry about our son having enough to eat because jails and prisons reportedly underfeed their inmates on purpose.

According to Prison Voice, an advocacy group in Washington State, prison inmates are fed on less than $1.20 a day. And by way of being punished for misbehavior, inmates are often made to eat reheated meatloaf at every meal for days, weeks and months at a time. Each institution creates their own recipe of the brownish lump, usually by throwing leftovers into a machine, creating a puree then adding starches with no seasoning. It's bland and it tastes like cardboard. One prisoner is quoted as saying, "I would have to be on the point of dizziness before I would eat it. There are a lot of cat food products prisoners would prefer to eat."

Privatization of our prisons also means more out-sourcing for food. This has led to pre-packaged meals, which use less fresh food and have much higher levels of sugar, salt, and trans-fats than traditional prison fare. In my opinion, breaking down a human's mental health and constitution by serving extremely limited food portions and unhealthy, sometimes inedible, food is cruel and unusual punishment.

Then when an inmate with a Traumatic Brain Injury is finally released, it's often challenging, if not impossible, for them to meet the current expectations of parole and probation. Even with family support, these people get arrested on a regular basis, and these souls are then at the mercy of guards who often appear to have no empathy for mentally and physically damaged inmates. Each arrest and incarceration is a traumatizing setback that deeply impacts a person's mental health, physical health and hard-earned progress.

When these inmates are eventually sent back into the world, they are often more mentally and physically ill than they were before they were locked up, like what happened to our boy.

These barbaric practices are tragic, heartbreaking, and need to be stopped.

Again, if TBI could be acknowledged in the courtroom, afflicted individuals would not be judged nor treated the same as criminals who have intent.

Out of the blue one day, our County Supervisor's secretary calls me and says, "Our Supervisor wants to convert an old local jail into a mental health lockdown facility in Ojai. Would you be willing to tell your son's story? You would be speaking to homeowners and business owners such as yourself."

When I arrive at our local paint store across the street from the old jail facility, I share our story and suggest a scenario where people who occupy a cell complete a mandatory rehabilitation program while being housed there. If medication is needed after diagnosis, the client is given the proper dosage with input from the individual, their guardian or both. Each cell could be rebuilt like a scaled down tiny home providing basic necessities–a bed, sink, toilet and amenities such as a desk and a dresser for clothing. Something they can take pride in, something that helps them keep in touch with the realities of modern life.

Working with the earth is considered one of the highest functioning therapies for people with TBI. Perhaps "sentencing" could mean mandatory time spent in the gardens if a person is mentally and physically able. These gardens would help provide a healthy diet for those in the program.

I did my best but am not surprised when the consensus of those at the County Supervisors meeting is not supportive. They conclude that business and real estate values would plummet if these folks were to be treated, housed and fed nearby.

As a business owner myself, I can understand this decision. But as a human, I have to wonder, how is it that our powerful, rich country cannot find the means to help those that cannot help themselves? Isn't there a saying about that? "Whatever you do for the least of these, you also do for me."

Right now in America, Traumatic Brain Injury will affect a loved one every twenty-one seconds.

CHAPTER 28

TOMMY'S WORLD

Every week when I drive into Ventura to do errands, it is with the hope of seeing Tommy. We often don't know his whereabouts but reason that he is likely still homeless. I stop at a red light that faces the white-washed walls of a Mediterranean-style house. Tall green palm trees cast dark silhouettes on the pristine white structure, like the black and white stripes of a Bengal tiger. Its purple neon sign blinking in the front window reads, "Palm Readings." Although I have no idea how a medium translates information from the psychic world into this realm, in my desperation, I wonder if a palm reader can give me any clues of Tommy's whereabouts.

Right after the light turns green, I find myself in the parking lot. I am at such a loss and feel so vulnerable, almost embarrassed. Is this what it looks like when desperate people do desperate things? Like entrusting the details of their lives to a roadside psychic?

Walking toward the entrance, my legs feel like they are filled with wet cement. I ring the bell. On the other side of the opaque glass, a figure wearing vibrant colors appears and opens the door. I am greeted by an older, regal-looking woman wrapped in a sheer purple gown, detailed with gold ribbon. She looks like an elegant Egyptian queen.

Sickened with apprehension, I don't know what to say, so she asks me, "Would you like to step inside?"

She closes the door and seals the whole world off behind me, except for the calming sound of water trickling over stones in her parlor. Settling in behind a large desk, she motions for me to take the chair closest to her.

"Normally no one is here unless someone is scheduled to be seen," she says, picking up a palm-sized piece of smooth quartz. "I am just here to pick up my mail."

"Thank you for opening your door and taking time with me. When I stopped at the red light across the street, I studied this house, and wondered if it might hold any insight for our family. I desperately need answers and direction regarding our brain-injured, homeless son."

My new spiritual advisor then tells me that I am trying too hard to make Tommy fit into my world.

"Maybe you might try visiting his world? Perhaps take him some clean socks, clothes, and food. See where he lives, meet his friends. Could you do this?"

My eyes instantly filling with tears, I can't get over the simplicity of her wisdom. When Tommy finally reaches out to us by telephone, he and I arrange to meet—in his world.

I forgot that the only way for me to get to Tommy's campsite is either through the train trestles or on the beach when the tide is out. As I approach the train tracks, I see Tommy's confident presence and beautiful smile. Any fear I have about finding my way instantly dissolves. We are so happy to see each other! He is over the moon excited when I hand him a large backpack that Tom and I had stuffed with clothing, food, water, and two big healthy sandwiches for us to eat that day.

Mentally he seems so present and sweet, but he is concerned about me crossing the trestles and carefully instructs me on how we were going to do it. Before embarking on the journey, I look down at the river feeding into the ocean and assess the situation. The tide is really high, and the water is a deep dark green color, fading to light green closer to the surface where the sun is shining through. The current is moving calmly, and if we absolutely have to jump because the train is coming through, I think the bridge is low enough and the water deep enough that though it would be terribly frightening, it would be doable. We both know I am a strong, confident swimmer, who as a child would swim and water ski in the ocean. When we reach the other side, I realize I had been holding my breath all the way across the bridge, and I'm just so thankful that we are on a different time schedule from the train!

Continuing on the trail toward Tommy's camp, I discover, in an ironic twist of fate—that a labyrinth of homeless camps is situated on one of the finest ocean front properties in California. Tall, dense clusters of green bamboo foliage create total privacy for the people nestled deep in their shade. Just a couple hundred feet from their camps, the Pacific Ocean crashes in a rhythmic tempo steadily on the shore. Trekking on little pathways through the towering stalks, we pass others who have carved out their own little camps in the thick vegetation.

Tommy greets them and introduces me by calling out, "This is my mom!" People are kind to us, saying hi to Tommy and greeting me with their broken smiles. Acutely aware that I have just shampooed my hair and put clean clothes on, it is in that moment that I have the realization of how alike we all are. We all have the same light in our eyes, and a heart beating in our chests. I think of the saying, "There but for the grace of god go I."

There is a kinship within the people I meet in the crooks and crags of that bamboo forest. I come to understand that Tommy is treated like a family member when he is living amongst these non-confrontational people. These are folks who mostly have little contact with their original families because of their struggles, and Tommy represents to them a lost brother, a son, a cousin, a friend. A natural empath, Tommy feels other people's pain and shares the abundance of love that he was shown throughout his childhood and into his adult life.

He even introduces me to his "street mom," who goes on and on about what a good person Tommy is and what a good job I am doing raising him and standing by his side.

Afterwards, back at Tommy's camp, he says, "She's not really my mom, Mom. You know I love you more, right?" I look up at him to see if he is being sincere, and he was! I just start laughing, as does he. He can be so sweet and silly sometimes.

Tommy crawls into his tent and begins taking out items from the backpack and placing them on his sleeping bag. He is so filled with anticipation and joy that it reminds me of his childhood holidays when he'd be taking one item at a time from his Easter Basket or Christmas stocking. Genuinely thrilled with each thing we packed for him, he's most excited to have a flashlight with extra batteries. "It gets soooo dark out here!"

Handing me a big sandwich he's taken from the backpack, he grins and says, "Mom, this looks great! I'm starving. Thank you...and please, thank Dad, too."

We eat in near silence, occasionally passing a water bottle back and forth. The ocean whispers in the distance, and all around I can hear muffled conversations from various campsites. I realize how many lives are held in the womb of this little forest. Tommy, eating pretty fast, gets up to look at all the bounty from his backpack that he strategically laid out on his bedding. Cinching up his tent with his new belongings inside, he asks, "Mom, can I walk you across the bridge?"

Meandering through the bamboo forest, we once again approach the train trestles. Step by step, one railroad tie at a time, we carefully return to the other side and say our heartfelt goodbyes. Coming back from another dimension, a parallel universe of vagabonds and misfits, a community of society's refugees, I feel something shift in me. Meeting Tommy in his world, as the psychic palm reader had suggested, was so right. Was it because I didn't try to change anything about his life? And that I wasn't sad when he showed me his "home"? Why didn't this make me yearn for a better life for him? Simply, it was because I got to share an afternoon of smiles, food, and connection with our son and his street family. The acceptance by a village of people who live with one another, but outside of society, gives me the courage to love unconditionally, and live my own life more authentically, and to "be the change I wish to see in the world."

EPILOGUE
OUR FAMILY LIVES ON

While Tommy's undiagnosed Traumatic Brain Injury has been running its course, our daughter, Lisa, has raised her four children. Occasionally she spends her time recording in our home studio with her younger sister Laurie and their dad. Lisa spends her days in the sun as a full-time hiking guide for the Ojai Valley Inn and hosts her brother, Tommy, for overnights when he's given permission from his sober living program.

Son Jeff married his high school sweetheart, Kasey, and while raising their two children, they've grown into entrepreneurs, designing and building their own award-winning family style Italian pizzeria. As their children grew older, Jeff and Kasey became part of Ojai's housing solution by buying land with two very small wooden houses on it. On that same land they built tiny houses using recycled materials and dub their project, *The Compound*. The Compound gets acknowledged in a progressive Japanese magazine showcasing its affordability and the need for Tiny Houses when space is limited.

Jeff, also a musician, invites his brother, Tommy, to play harmonica on some of his songs and helps Tommy whenever he can. He and Kasey are their happiest being grandparents to their new grandson, and our first great-grandson, Zevi.

After graduating college, Ted left California for the New York music scene. After busking in subways and honing his skills, Ted returned home and asked his much-missed sweetheart, Amber, to marry him. After she gave birth to their first-born son Charlie, Ted asked his dad to record with him on his first album.

They recorded on a vintage reel-to-reel tape recorder in our floor-to-ceiling wooden living room, creating perfect recording acoustics. Tom added guitar, ukulele and back-up vocals, and the album was a critical success, leading to a recording contract with Universal Music Japan. Ted and Amber were soon blessed with a baby girl named Hazel. Today, Ted's music has millions of streams on all the major streaming platforms, he just finished a West Coast tour, and he recently opened for Vieux Farka Toure, West African musician and son of the legendary Ali Farka Toure.

With fairy dust scattered over a multiplicity of strengths, our youngest, Laurie Beth, helps keep her brother, Tommy's, spirits up with her humor and their laughter. She'll often give insightful and practical feedback to Tommy when he asks for it, which helps him with his decision making.

A natural born actress, dancer and comedian, she eventually married another actor, Dwier Brown, who is best known for playing John Kinsella, Kevin Costner's dad, in the movie *Field of Dreams*. Laurie is Dwier's agent, public relations person, marketer and wardrobe fashionista. Dwier also wrote a book all about fatherhood and baseball called *If You Build It*. With a growing fanbase every year, Dwier tours around the country for speaking engagements and public appearances. They are currently building a Baseball Museum not far from the movie location in Iowa.

When not in Iowa or on the road, they spend their time together at home in Ojai. Laurie and Dwier have two grown children, a son and a daughter, and now a son-in-law.

Tommy's boy, Elijah, wanting a college education but not able to afford one, decided to join the U.S. Army and served our country for two years. In return, the government paid for Elijah's education and housing. Elijah graduated college and received a degree in Criminal Justice and has chosen to dedicate his life's work to assisting under-privileged families. He guides them and other less fortunate people through the social service benefits they are all so desperately in need of. His Daddy is very proud. So are we.

After husband Tom worked with the Pioneer French Baking Company for twenty years, he took an early retirement in his late forties, and we never looked back.

When he is not singing and playing his guitar at our local farmer's market, different wineries and on stages with his larger Lennon family, he works on his own guitars and helps repair wooden instruments and collectible tube amplifiers for our family and friends. And because necessity is the mother of invention, Tom has a patent on a tool holder, which he invented for his luthier work.

Tom continues to be dedicated to the use of neurofeedback electrodes and exploring which areas of stimulation are most helpful to Tommy. He also continues to converse with neurofeedback doctors and practitioners online daily.

In our late 1800s creek-side cottage, my red violin, a family heirloom, hangs on a wall and occasionally calls out to me to come warm it up. I stay healthy by walking daily and gardening. In the summertime when water temperatures are warmer, our family will head down to the ocean to swim, picnic and play volleyball.

I'm mostly retired from my vintage clothing shop in Ojai. The Lennon Closet is in its fourteenth year of business and remains open due to dear friends and customers who make it possible for us to continue contributing a percentage of our yearly sales to our most relevant charity, B.R.A.I.N. (Brain Rehabilitation and Injury Network).

Writing this book, sharing my thoughts and feelings, telling Tommy's story has been one of the major accomplishments of my life.

And Tommy? Where's Tommy?

All throughout his forties and in between incarcerations and homelessness, Tommy has been actively selling his artwork on recycled clothing, filming another documentary and lining up speaking engagements. While living and thriving at a local program called Freedom House, he began to exhibit some sadly familiar behavior. "If only I could be free from all of these program rules...told when to wake up, when I can lay down on my bed and relax, what time I have to be home at night...there's so many limitations, I can't even remember the last time I went surfing or swam in the ocean because I can't submerge this ankle tracker in water!"

Impulsively, Tommy once again left the good life he'd worked so hard for. Over two months passed without hearing from Tommy and going that length of time was a first for us all!

Then out of thin air, we get an email from Tommy's attorney. They've found Tommy in Los Angeles. He's in custody in Ventura on a probation violation. Instantly our grief is turned on its head, and we feel relief like we've never felt before.

Finally, we hear from Tommy. "This is a free call from an incarcerated inmate..."

"Hello?"

"Tommy!!! OHHH! It's so good to hear your voice!!! You're on speaker, so that dad can hear you too!"

"Hi, Dad!"

"Hi, Tommy! How are you?"

"Yeah, I don't know what happened. It was pretty bad, there are some real haters out there. I thought some guy was my friend and just wanted to clown around and play fight with me...I have no idea why he punched me in the face so hard, it broke my nose and loosened four of my teeth! Do you know when I might get outta here?"

Barely able to stomach what he just told us, we answer with, "No, we don't."

"I have to get off the phone and lock it down. I love you guys so much."

"We love you too, Tommy."

As we hang up the phone, Mr. Simpson, the owner of Tommy's live-in program calls us.

"Hi, how are you two? I just got an update from Tommy's mental health team. Tommy will be released to my care the day after tomorrow. Tom, if you and Debbie can get documentation from the TBI doctor you've spoken to regarding Tommy's impulsivity, I'll try everything in my power to make sure Tommy never goes to jail or prison again."

Thanking Simpson, I ask him out of curiosity, "Are you this dedicated to all of your clients?"

"I am dedicated to my clients, have been for twenty-five years. I love what I do! But I dunno, when it comes to Tommy, he's a good guy, funny as hell. I just love him." Suddenly overcome by emotion, Simpson's voice breaks, "Working for so many months with Tommy, then him taking off, it broke my heart. I could see he wanted *it* so badly."

There ARE good people out there who are trying to help. The problem is identifying what is best for Tommy. I recall a conversation we had with him during one of his incarcerations...

He was eager to see us. Picking up our telephones he greeted us through the thick plated glass with a warm hello and the lingering question, "Am I going to be housed when I get out?"

"You can return to Casa Esperanza in Camarillo or the Camp in Oxnard. That's what we have."

He looked tired. Gutted. It's as though the fabric of his constitution was no longer tightly woven.

"Honestly, the thought of getting out of here and starting over sounds so overwhelming! I've been doing homelessness and jail for too long. I mean, I just spent my 53rd birthday in here," Tommy slumped forward with his hands placed together shaped in prayer. "Everything sounds too hard to face right now. I must be institutionalized cuz everything on the outside feels too complicated. Everything in here is already taken care of. With your and Dad's help, I can eat when I am hungry, I have shelter, and I can take a bath and get both my legs and feet wet because I don't have to wear a tracking monitor. I have my own jail cell that I don't have to share with anyone like I do when I'm outside."

His face shows all the years of struggle and abuse. "I've had a horrible life."

His words hang in the air, begging to be refuted.

Tom and I, both deeply saddened by this truth, agreed in unison, "Yes, you have."

But then his desire for freedom would resurface. One day, we have a remarkable phone conversation with him...

At home, absorbed in thought over Tommy's dilemma, my cell phone rings, and I hear a recording that's all too familiar.

"This is a free call from, (we hear Tommy say his name), an incarcerated inmate at Ventura County Jail. This call will be monitored and recorded. If you feel there has been an error and this should be a private call, please hang up and try again. To accept this free call press one, to no longer receive calls from this facility press two."

BEEEEEP! I press the first option and hear Tommy's voice beam through the telephone.

"Mom!! I miss you!"

"Hi, Tommy! I miss you too."

"Would you and Dad please help me end this chapter in my life, forever? You don't have to say yes or no right now. But I hope you and Dad will think about helping me with what I'm calling, My Practical Plan. Mom, can you get a pen and paper and write down what needs to happen?"

I find a piece of paper and a pen and tell Tommy I'm ready.

"Great! Thanks, Mom. Number one, call a TBI lawyer."

"Ok, got it."

"Two, get documented proof of the frontal lobe injury to my head."

"Not so fast! Ok, I've got it."

"Three, get a TBI doctor that can explain to a judge that the impulse control area of my brain has been injured."

"WAIT!"

"What mom?"

"Tommy, who helped you organize this list?"

"What do you mean?"

"How did you come up with this list, Tommy?"

"What are you talking about Mom!! I have nothing on my hands but time to think! No one helped me make this list. Please, keep writing, I only have a few minutes before I have to lock it down."

As I continue to write, I'm shaking my head back and forth in total disbelief, still wondering, *how did he come up with this on his own?* Tommy continues and I notate the remaining steps of Tommy's plan:

4. Get my case put on the calendar ASAP.

5. My TBI is finally addressed through the court with a request that my parole be terminated due to TBI.

6. After we clear up parole, then we clean up my record so that I no longer have to register on my birthday. I pleaded guilty when I should have never pled guilty.

7. I need a Civil Rights Attorney that will address:

a) All the abuse and added head injuries due to continuous arrests.

b) Injuries from holding me down on many occasions to administer medications against my will, which had not been processed through the courts.

c) Reinstating my Supplemental Security Income after all the years of being declined and letting it support my housing and personal needs.

"Did you write it all down?" Tommy asks.

"I got it!"

"Read it back to me, please!"

I read his list back to him as Tom is listening in.

"Can I say hi to Dad?"

While handing Tom the phone, the jail P.A. system tells the prisoners to, "Lock it down!" Tommy, knowing he has to return to his cell immediately, quickly says, "I gotta go Dad, I love you!"

"I love you too, Tommy."

Tom and I look at each other. We can hardly believe that Tommy wrote that list himself! Where did this lucid plan come from? Was it the number of back-to-back arrests and the repeated serving of 180-day jail sentences that finally got through to Tommy? Was it the information repeated to him by judges for more than three decades? Is it behaving in the same way, getting arrested for the same violations and getting the same results, that is allowing this information to finally become available to his executive brain? Or is it a sign of progress?

It's at moments like this that we remember the remarkable young man that he once was. The one that so many people labeled special. He still is all that.

And now Tommy will be going back to Freedom House again. We will visit and do everything that we can to help. We will continue to work on his Practical Plan.

When the phone rings, we will always answer.

"Mom, it's Tommy! Are you and Dad coming out to see me?"

Yes, Tommy. We will...

THE END

ACKNOWLEDGEMENTS

I didn't write this book because I set out to be a writer or because I thought I'd win a Pulitzer Prize for my masterfulness. I wrote the book because a command rose up within me that I couldn't ignore—an inner assignment to tell the truth at all costs.

Ten years later, this labor of love has been completed. It is my true belief that this book wouldn't have come to see the light of day without the incredible village of countless individuals. Thankfully, I have the tremendous blessing of family, which plays a crucial role in every aspect of my life, including the writing of this book. A deep bow of gratitude to the team of family editors & beta readers who helped turn my creative storytelling into a real memoir that captures the truths, tragedy and beauty I had hoped to convey. Amber Lennon, Billy & Gail Lennon, Laurie & Dwier Brown—you are the backbone of this book. I want to thank my husband Tom, who not only helped write and edit this book, but also has been my rock through the good times, the not so good times, and the tragic events that brought this memoir into being. I love you, Tom, with my whole heart.

Thank you to Gary Peattie, Linda Gravenson, Sonia Nordenson and Kia Penso (and Deb Norton for introducing us) for your editing genius and for believing in the value of getting our story out into the world. Jack Kindle & Stephanie Ballard, thank you for your lifelong friendship and intelligent literary feedback.

And to the team at Publishing Hackers, we couldn't have done it without your guidance, patience, creativity and practical knowledge of the publishing world. Brian, Whale, Michael, Tatiana—we thank each of you for the talent and professionalism you brought to our book.

After almost four decades through California's criminal justice and mental health systems, I'd like to thank all the kind professionals in those fields who assisted Tommy and have been literal angels in his life and ours. I can't thank each of you enough who stood up for truth and humanity in the face of a corrupt and failing system. My prayer is that this book comforts countless families with a loved one living with Traumatic Brain Injury. May it be a voice for all those suffering in silence, without legal representation, or even awareness that their life's dysfunction is due to TBI. I'm here to ring the bell of truth into the courtrooms and jails throughout America, into the hearts and minds of all those in positions of power and influence to make a change for the better.

Helpful Nonprofits

The below nonprofits are dedicated to improving the lives of TBI survivors and their families, and all donations received are used for this goal. If readers would like to donate or otherwise support these nonprofit organizations, please visit the QR code at the back of the book for links.

1. National Alliance for the Mentally Ill (N.A.M.I): dedicated to building better lives for people struggling with mental illness
   www.nami.org
   Ventura Chapter: www.namiventura.org

2. Brain Rehabilitation and Injury Network (B.R.A.I.N.): gives therapy for those who have been injured by brain injury
   www.thebrainsite.org
   5656 Corporate Ave
   Cypress, CA 90630

3. Strength in Pain Foundation: provides continuing awareness and education about Traumatic Brain Injury and Head Injury & access to treatments for those that are financially burdened by the costs
   www.strengthinpainfoundation.com
   394 Ogle Street Unit C
   Costa Mesa, CA 92627

Author Bio

Debbie Lennon is an advocate in the fields of Traumatic Brain Injury, the mentally ill, and the Armed Forces, bridging these areas with the criminal system and calling for reform. Debbie has been changing laws and improving people's lives for nearly forty years.

A Revolving Door, a short documentary about her son Tommy's traumatic brain injury, was short-listed for an Academy Award and aired on HBO. Debbie was asked to be a guest on the Oprah Winfrey show on three separate occasions.

Part of The National Alliance for the Mentally Ill, Debbie was asked to travel and look into housing for their clients. Writing down pertinent suggestions she felt the Board and Care facilities could benefit from, what stood out to her most was the severe housing shortage for people with mental disabilities, stating, "There's a whole homeless nation not housed."

Lennon's voice of experience represented The National Alliance for the Mentally Ill (NAMI) in helping win a $206 billion settlement against the major American tobacco companies. The money compensates forty-six states for health care costs from treating smoking related illnesses.

NAMI asked Debbie to speak on a new concept called Laura's Law. She became a main influencer bringing the concept to the forefront. Laura's Law was passed and has been helping a small population of individuals who meet strict legal criteria as a result of their mental illness that leaves them unable to voluntarily access mental health services.

An elected official contacted Debbie and asked her to speak about the need for an additional mental health lockdown facility, converting a recently emptied jail into a living and treatment facility for the mentally ill.

Debbie also helped create a trial program for the homeless, setting up a temporary camp where judges came to the homeless to dismiss their warrants for arrests for minor infractions, such as camping illegally. The program effectively mitigated an exponential number of arrests that fill jails and prisons with the downtrodden on a regular basis.

Asked to teach at a Crisis Intervention Training Program for law enforcement, Debbie explained how quickly police escalate the mentally ill into physical altercations ending in injury, arrests, and sometimes death. Debbie taught officers how to approach a mentally ill person who is fearful, and how to respond to them differently than how they respond to criminals with intent.

At a very successful Think Tank Program hosted by Brain Rehabilitation and Injury Network (B.R.A.I.N.), Debbie showed her documentary film and participated in a Q&A to a venue filled to capacity.

For over a decade, Debbie's fine consignment store, The Lennon Closet, in Ojai, California, has been recycling, selling, and exchanging reusable collectibles and vintage clothing, donating one percent of Debbie's annual sales to the B.R.A.I.N. nonprofit.

Having spent the first year of her marriage with her husband Tom as a military wife in Fort Riley, Kansas, Debbie has seen and researched the many challenges military people face after returning home from a combat zone. Debbie has become a voice for our heroes by advocating regularly for greater understanding of undiagnosed Traumatic Brain Injuries.

Debbie's biggest passion is her large family. Married for sixty years, Debbie and Tom actively enjoy their five children, their spouses, eleven grandchildren, and the newest addition to the family—a great-grand-son. Debbie Lennon lives and works in Ojai, California.

To learn more about TBI and support TBI nonprofits,
scan the QR code or go to the URL below:

linktr.ee/wherestommybook